This book belongs to

_____

Given by _____

Date _____

Blessings Every Day

365 SIMPLE DEVOTIONS FOR THE VERY YOUNG

Written by Carla Barnhill
Illustrated by Elena Kucharik

CANDLE BOOKS

First published in UK 2002 by Candle Books.
Distributed by STL, PO Box 300, Carlisle CA3 0QS.
Worldwide co-edition organised and produced by
Angus Hudson Ltd, Concorde House, Grenville Place,
Mill Hill, London NW7 3SA
Tel: +44 208 959 3668   Fax: +44 208 959 3678
e-mail: coed@angushudson.com

Printed in Singapore

Note to Parents

Like all parents, your goal is to do everything you can to produce healthy, happy children – who will become healthy, happy adults. And *Blessings Every Day* can help.

Each day features a Bible promise or truth, a short devotional based on an age-appropriate theme, and a whimsical rhyme capturing the day's truth with lighthearted charm. The heartwarming illustrations by well-known and loved illustrator Elena Kucharik, who created the Care bears, are tailor-made to engage even the youngest child – and delight you, as a parent, too!

Blessings Every Day is a lively adventure – a walk through the Bible, Genesis through Revelations – where your children can discover for themselves who God is, his many rich promises, and how those promises relate to us today.

About the Illustrator

Elena Kucharik has been a freelance illustrator for over twenty-five yeard. During this time she was the lead artist and developer of the well-known Care Bears. For over ten years Elena has been focusing her talents on illustrations for children's books, including creating the Little Blessings characters. Elena and her husband live in New Canaan, Connecticut, and have two grown daughters.

About the Writer

Carla Barnhill, a busy mum with two young children, has a master;s degree in literature from the University of Edinburgh in Scotland and a bachelor's degree from Concordia College in Minnesota. Formerly she was managing director of *Christian Parenting Today* magazine and is one of the general editors of the *Teen Devotional Bible* (Zondervan). She, her husband, and their children live in the Chicago area.

January

God's Favourite Creation

God created the heavens and the earth.
Genesis 1:1, NIV

Do you like to play with clay or build with bricks? Isn't it fun to create funny shapes and tall towers? Imagine how much fun God had making fish and mountains and stars and rivers! God made everything, from the moon high in the sky to the wiggly worms deep in the ground. But his favourite creation of all is you!

God made everything I can see.
And best of all, he made me!

Look-Alikes

God created people in his own image.
Genesis 1:27, NLT

God made lots of different kinds of people! We come in all shapes and sizes and colours. Even in your own family, nobody looks exactly the same. But no matter how different we look, we are all part of God's family. Of all the things God made when he created the world, people are the most special.

God made everyone, both you and me.
We are all part of his family.

Wild Things

God made all sorts of wild animals.
Genesis 1:25, TLB

The next time you go for a walk in the woods or take a trip to the zoo, see how many different kinds of animals you can find. There are deer and dragonflies, lions and leopards, seals and snakes—and that's just the beginning! There are more animals in the world than could possibly fit in one place. And God made every single one of them. If he can make bears and bugs, there's nothing he can't do.

God made all of the birds that soar,
God made all of the lions that roar!

Fantastic You

God saw all that he had made, and it was very good.
Genesis 1:31, NIV

Have you ever felt like nobody likes you? We all have days when we feel ignored or picked on or left out. But do you know who thinks you're amazing every single minute of every single day? God does! After God finished making everything in the world, he looked it over and liked what he saw. The next time you feel like nobody likes you, remember that God thinks you're fantastic!

When God looks at me,
He likes what he sees.

The Rainbow Promise

*I have placed my rainbow in the clouds
as a sign of my promise until the end of time.*
Genesis 9:13, *TLB*

Where did rainbows come from? A long time ago, a big flood covered the whole earth with water. After the flood, God put a beautiful rainbow in the sky as a promise to people that there would never be a flood like that again. Every rainbow is a special reminder of God's love for us.

God sent us rainbows to show us he cares.
Whenever we see one, we know that he's there.

All We Need

I will bless you with incredible blessings.
Genesis 22:17, TLB

Have you ever begged your mum or dad to buy you something at the shops? Sometimes we think we need more than what we have. But God really has given us all kinds of wonderful things. We have families who love us, friends to play with, food to eat, and houses to keep us safe and warm. That's a lot to be happy about!

Help me be happy for all that you give,
Family and friends and a safe place to live.

Never Alone

I am with you and will watch over you wherever you go.
Genesis 28:15, NIV

When you were a tiny baby, you were with your mum or dad almost all the time. Now that you're growing bigger, you can go exciting places on your own. Maybe you get to spend the night at your friend's house. At bedtime, though, you might feel a little lonely without your parents to tuck you in. But God is with you no matter where you go. Even though you can't see him, God is everywhere you are, watching over you.

Wherever I wander, wherever I roam,
God is with me, so I'm never alone.

Don't Be Shy

I will help you speak and will teach you what to say.
Exodus 4:12, NIV

Do you ever feel so shy that you can't say a word? Especially around people you don't know? When you meet someone new, remember that God will help you speak up. You don't have to worry about what to say. Just smile your biggest smile and say hello. Before you know it, you won't feel shy anymore!

When I feel shy, I have nothing to say.
But God helps me speak in my very own way!

Thanks, Mum and Dad!

Honour your father and mother.
Exodus 20:12, NLT

Your parents do all kinds of nice things for you. They take good care of you. They work hard so you'll have everything you need. They read to you and teach you new things. You can show them you love them by doing nice things for them too. You can listen to them, do what they ask without complaining, and help them all you can. And giving them a hug is a great way to say thanks!

Thanks for my parents—a gift from above.
Help me to give them all of my love.

Accidents Happen

The Lord is slow to anger and rich in unfailing love.
Numbers 14:18, NLT

It's easy to get upset when someone hurts you or breaks something that belongs to you. But God wants us to follow his example and be patient with other people. So when your little brother takes your building bricks or your sister loses your favourite teddy bear, remember that God is patient with us when we do things we shouldn't. He wants us to treat others the same way.

God, help me be patient whenever I'm mad.
I know when I'm patient, it makes you so glad.

Warm Hearts

Love the Lord your God with all your heart, soul and strength.
Deuteronomy 6:5, ICB

When you love someone, your whole heart is full of warm feelings. And it's fun to tell the people you love how you feel. When you love God, your whole heart fills up with good feelings. God does wonderful things for you. Be sure to tell him how you feel.

God, I love you with all of my heart.
Knowing you love me is the very best part.

A Letter from God

Remember my words in your hearts and souls.
Deuteronomy 11:18, ICB

The Bible is like a great big letter from God. In the Bible God tells us all the important things he wants us to know. He tells us about himself. He tells us how to follow him and how much he loves us. Most of all, he tells us about his Son, Jesus. It's fun to read the Bible—it's like reading a letter from your very best friend.

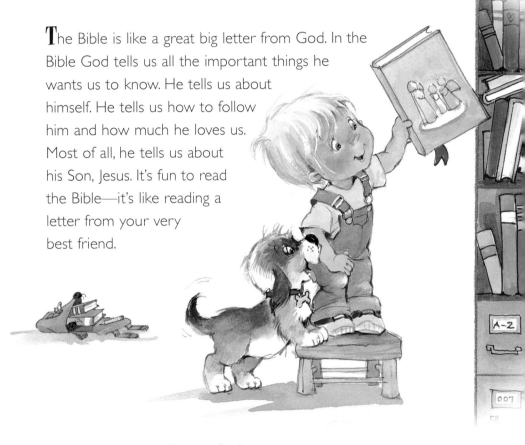

The Bible is God's special letter to me.
It helps me to see all he wants me to be.

Only God

There is none like God.
Deuteronomy 33:26, NRSV

Think fast! Do you know anyone who can create an ocean? Or make the sun? Or build a person out of dust? Well, God can. He can do anything. Best of all, God promises to take care of us forever. Isn't it great to have someone so awesome and powerful watching out for us?

You made the world, both the land and the sea,
And you promise always to take care of me.

Safe and Sound

The everlasting God is your place of safety.
Deuteronomy 33:27, ICB

What do you do when you're scared? Do you hide behind your dad or your mum? Do you run to your room or pull a blanket over your head? All of those things can help you feel safe. But even when your parents aren't around or you can't find a place to hide, remember God can do anything. And he promises to always keep you safe.

When I get scared, I know God is there.
He keeps me safe in his loving care.

God Is There

I will never leave you alone.
Joshua 1:5, ICB

The Bible is full of stories about people doing amazing things. Take Joshua, for instance. God asked him to lead a huge group of people into an unknown place. Pretty scary, huh? But God promised Joshua that he'd take care of him and help him every step of the way. And God did just that!

God is with me wherever I go.
I know it's true. He tells me so.

Strong and Brave

Remember that I commanded you to
be strong and brave. So don't be afraid.
Joshua 1:9, ICB

It's not easy to be brave, is it? But God wants us to trust him to take care of us. When we have to do something scary, we can ask God to help us be brave, and he will. So the next time you have to tell the truth even though you might get in trouble, or the next time you go somewhere new without your parents, remember that God will be with you, helping you to be strong and brave.

I am brave with God by my side.
I am strong—I don't have to hide.

Sing a Song

I will sing to the Lord.
Judges 5:3, NIV

There's just something about singing that makes you feel good. When you're sad, a sweet song from someone you love can help you feel better. When you're happy, you can't help but sing a cheerful song. God loves to hear us sing to him. Whether it's "Jesus Loves Me" or something you make up all by yourself, sing a song for God today.

I know that God loves it when I sing a song.
I'll sing about loving him all the day long.

A Solid Rock

There is no Rock like our God.
1 Samuel 2:2, NIV

Do you like to collect rocks? Rocks come in all different sizes, and they're pretty amazing. Have you ever tried to break one? They're really strong. Big rocks are great to stand on when you want to see higher or sit on when you need to rest. That's why the Bible calls God a rock. God is incredibly strong, and he's always there when we need him. Pretty amazing!

God is our rock. He's solid and strong.
Whenever we trust him, we'll never go wrong.

Peekaboo

People look at the outside of a person, but the Lord looks at the heart.
I Samuel 16:7, ICB

What's the first thing people see when they look at you? Your freckles? Your curly hair? Your big smile? Whatever people see when they look at you, it's only a little piece of what makes you *you*. But when God looks at you, he sees everything about you, like how friendly or smart or kind you are. Most of all, God sees the wonderful person he made. And that's what he loves most.

God sees inside me, he sees in my heart.
To him I am wonderful, lovely, and smart!

A Bright Light

O Lord, you are my light! You make my darkness bright.
2 Samuel 22:29, TLB

Tonight, ask your mum or dad to turn out all the lights in your room. It gets very dark, doesn't it? Then ask them to turn the lights back on. What happens now? Your room is full of light again. That's what God is like. Just knowing God loves us makes our whole world bright.

God's love is so bright,
It can light up the night!

The Promise Keeper

All the Lord's promises prove true.
2 Samuel 22:31, NLT

Has anyone ever broken a promise he or she made to you? Maybe a friend told you he'd play with you and then changed his mind. Or maybe your mum promised to take you to the park, then got busy doing something else and couldn't. Even when people don't mean to break their promises, it still hurts.

God makes a lot of promises in the Bible. He promises he will always take care of us. He promises to love us forever. He promises that someday we'll live with him in heaven. And God keeps every single one of his promises. You can count on it.

God keeps his promises, I know it's true.
He promises always to love me and you.

No Matter What

He will constantly look after my safety and success.
2 Samuel 23:5, NLT

King David was a man who did many great things and also some bad things. But at the end of his life, he knew God had been with him every day. He knew God loved him, even when he made bad choices and big mistakes. And just like God loved David, he loves and cares for all of us.

Good or bad, whatever we do—
God still cares, his love is still true.

Doing Right

Give me wisdom.... Help me know what is right and what is wrong.
1 Kings 3:9, TSLB

Some choices are easy, like what you want to eat. But other choices are harder. Should you tell your mum you accidentally broke her favourite flowerpot? We need God's help to make good choices. When we ask for his help, he'll show us what to do. And he'll give us the strength to do what's right.

God can help me make good choices each day.
Whenever I ask him, he'll show me the way.

God's Wonderful World

Remember the wonderful things [God] has done.
1 Chronicles 16:12, ICB

The world is full of good things God made, like trees, flowers, grass, birds, and sunshine. Isn't it fun to squish your toes in the mud? Or splash in a puddle? Or catch frosty snowflakes on your tongue? God made all these things so we would be happy. What a wonderful world! What a wonderful God!

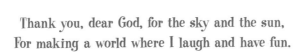

Thank you, dear God, for the sky and the sun,
For making a world where I laugh and have fun.

Big Jobs

Don't be frightened by the size of the task,
for the Lord my God is with you.
1 Chronicles 28:20, TLB

Solomon was a young man who had a big job to do. And he was nervous about it! But his father, David, reminded him that no job is too big for God. With God by his side, Solomon learned he could do anything. The next time you have a big job to do, ask for God's help. With him, you can do anything too.

No matter how big I think the job is,
God will help me, and I know I am his.

Follow the Leader

*You are the God who keeps his kind promises to all those who obey you
and who are anxious to do your will.*
2 Chronicles 6:14, *TLB*

God keeps all his promises to us, no matter what. And he wants
us to promise to follow him
and do what he asks.
He wants us to be
kind to others, listen
to our parents, and try
our best to do what's right.
When we obey God, we
show him how much we
love him and how glad
we are to be his children.

God, you are good. You do all that you say.
Help me to love you and always obey.

Now Hear This

Then my people, who are called by my name, will be sorry for what they have done. They will pray and . . . I will hear them from heaven.
2 Chronicles 7:14, ICB

God's got the whole world to look after, and that's a *very* big job. But when you have a problem, God is right there to listen and help. That's true even when you've done something wrong and want to talk to God about it. No matter how busy God is, he always has time for you.

When I'm in trouble, I give God a call.
He hears all my problems, the big and the small.

Who Loves You?

[God] is good; his love for Israel continues forever.
Ezra 3:11, ICB

If you look at a map of the world, you can find a country called Israel. But when the Bible uses the word *Israel*, it means *all* of God's people. So when the Bible says God's love for Israel goes on forever, it means that God loves *you* forever! Doesn't that feel great?

I'm one of God's people for all of my days.
He shows me his love in all kinds of ways.

Pizza and Pancakes

The joy of the Lord is your strength.
Nehemiah 8:10, NIV

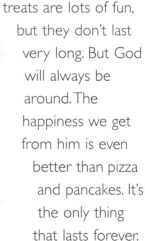

Imagine a day when you have chocolate chip pancakes for breakfast, play at the park all morning, and eat pizza and ice cream for lunch. And then you spend the rest of the day playing with your favourite toys. What a great day! Toys and treats are lots of fun, but they don't last very long. But God will always be around. The happiness we get from him is even better than pizza and pancakes. It's the only thing that lasts forever.

If I want the joy that will last in my heart,
A friendship with God is the best place to start.

God Is Everywhere

You give life to everything, and the multitudes of heaven worship you.
Nehemiah 9:6, NIV

We think about God when we go to church or read the Bible. But God is everywhere. Even though we can't see him, we can see lots of things he made. So the next time you're outside, look around your neighbourhood. Think about who made all the things you see. The trees, the birds, the clouds all come from God. Everywhere you look, you can think about God and thank him for making such an awesome world.

You made the sky and the trees and the birds.
Help me to thank you with wonderful words.

What Is God Like?

You are a God of forgiveness, gracious and merciful, slow to become angry, and full of unfailing love and mercy.
Nehemiah 9:17, NLT

Since we can't see God, it's hard to understand what he's like. But this Bible verse tells us he's everything we could ever want in a friend. He always forgives us when we do something wrong, he's slow to get angry with us, he understands what it's like to be a kid, and, most of all, he loves us more than we can even imagine. What a fantastic friend!

Dear God, you're really my best-of-all friend.
And your love for me will never end.

February

Jump for Joy!

He will yet fill your mouth with laughter and your lips with shouts of joy.
Job 8:21, NIV

Do you ever let out a big "Yippee!" when you're excited? When you're really happy about something, you can't keep all that happiness inside. Every day is full of happy things that make you want to jump for joy. A hug from your mum, running as fast as you can, or eating an ice-cream cone—what else can you think of?

When I am happy I laugh and I shout—
The joy that I'm feeling just has to jump out!

Yesterday, Today, and Tomorrow

You gave me life and showed me kindness.
And in your care you watched over my life.
Job 10:12, ICB

Job, the man who said these words in the Bible, was going through a very hard time. But even though he was having lots of problems, Job still trusted God to take care of him. He thought about all the good things God had done in his life. He knew that God had helped him in the past and would help him in the future, too. And God will do the same for you!

God is with me every day.
He always helps me find my way.

FEBRUARY 3

Who Knows?

But true wisdom and power are God's.
He alone knows what we should do; he understands.
Job 12:13, TLB

Have you ever had a hard time making a choice between right and wrong? Maybe a friend asked you to tell a lie, or someone teased you and you were tempted to tease them back. God will always help you make the right decision. Just ask for his help, and he'll show you the right thing to do.

God always knows just what I should do.
He'll always help me, and he'll always help you.

Count on God

I know that you can do all things.
Job 42:12, NIV

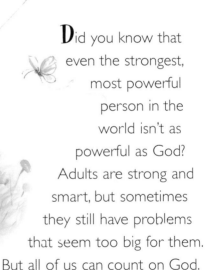

Did you know that
even the strongest,
most powerful
person in the
world isn't as
powerful as God?
Adults are strong and
smart, but sometimes
they still have problems
that seem too big for them.
But all of us can count on God.
So when you have a problem you can't solve,
ask God to help. Remember, he can do anything!

God, you are big—you're the strongest of all!
I know you will help me whenever I call.

Sleep Tight

I will lie down and sleep in peace.
Psalm 4:8, NIV

God watches over you all day long, no matter where you go. But did you know God even watches out for you while you sleep? You don't have to be scared of the dark or worry about having bad dreams. Just remember that God is with you, making sure you're safe all night long.

God watches over me all through the night,
Making sure that I always sleep tight.

Good Morning, God!

Lord, every morning you hear my voice. . . . I tell you what I need,
and I wait for your answer.
Psalm 5:3, ICB

What's the first thing you do in the morning? Do you eat breakfast or brush your teeth or snuggle with your parents? No matter how you start your day, don't forget to say good morning to God. Tell him about the day ahead. Tell him what you're excited about or nervous about or happy about. Remember, God's been with you all night long, and he can't wait to hear from you!

In the morning, I will say
Thank you, God, for this new day!

Strong Armour

You protect him with your shield of love.
Psalm 5:12, TLB

When soldiers in Bible times went to battle, they always carried shields to protect themselves. How else could they stay safe from the rocks and arrows their enemies might throw at them? We might not have to hide from rocks and arrows, but we all have scary things to face. It's a good thing we have God's love to protect us. It's a shield that will always keep us safe.

**Because God's love is all around me
A shield of safety will surround me.**

Always Safe

The Lord is my rock. . . . I can run to him for safety.
Psalm 18:2, ICB

God always wants you to be safe. Your parents do too. They do everything they can to take care of you. Your mum dresses you warmly when it's cold outside. Your dad holds your hand when you cross a busy street. If your parents have to go somewhere, they ask someone they trust to stay with you. You can trust both your parents and God to keep you safe.

My mum, my dad, and God makes three.
Together they take good care of me!

Trust God

Some trust in chariots, others in horses. But we trust the Lord our God.
Psalm 20:7, ICB

We all like new clothes, good food, and lots of toys. And God wants us to enjoy all these things. But he doesn't want us to be happy only if we have nice things. He wants us to be happy because he loves us, no matter how much or how little we own. And when we trust him, we'll have everything we need, forever!

Though I like lots of clothes and toys—
God's love and care are my biggest joys.

Little Lambs

Because the Lord is my Shepherd, I have everything I need!
Psalm 23:1, TLB

The Bible talks a lot about Jesus, God's Son, being our shepherd. It sounds funny since we're not sheep. But when the Bible says Jesus is our shepherd, it means that he takes care of us. A shepherd makes sure his sheep have good food to eat and a warm place to sleep. He stays awake at night to keep wolves away from his flock. He keeps them happy and safe both day and night. And just like a good shepherd, Jesus cares for us, too.

You are the shepherd—I am your lamb.
You keep me safe wherever I am.

Close beside Me

I will not be afraid, for you are close beside me,
guarding, guiding all the way.
Psalm 23:4, TLB

Whenever the Queen goes somewhere, lots of people go with her. Their job is to protect the Queen and make sure she's always safe. She's very important, and no one wants her to get hurt. God is always with you, too, wherever you go. He thinks you're so important that he wants to keep you safe all day and all night!

God, you protect me wherever I go.
You're always beside me—you won't let me go.

My Future

Surely goodness and love will follow me all the days of my life.
Psalm 23:6, *NIV*

What do you think life will be like in the future? What will you grow up to be? Where will you live? Nobody really knows what the future will be like. But we know that whatever happens, God will be there, taking care of us and watching over us.

**Because of you, God, my future looks bright.
Your love and your goodness make everything right.**

Have No Fear!

The Lord protects my life. I am afraid of no one.
Psalm 27:1, ICB

Life is full of new people, places, and things. At first you might feel afraid to meet someone new, to go somewhere you've never been before, or to try something different.

But remember, you don't have to be afraid of anything. You can be happy and enjoy all that life offers you!

With God at my side, I have nothing to fear.
He promises me he will always be near.

A Gift for God

Love the Lord, all you who belong to him.
Psalm 31:23, ICB

God does so many great things for us that it's nice when we can do something for him, too. But what could God need? Well, God does want something from us—our love. We show God our love when we talk to him, when we trust him to help us, and when we obey him. Show God you love him today.

God, help me show you I love you each day,
By all that I do and by all that I say.

A Fresh Start

Crying may last for a night, but joy comes in the morning.
Psalm 30:5, ICB

Some days are hard. You might feel grumpy. Or maybe you just can't seem to stay out of trouble. But God gives you a chance to start over again every morning. No matter how bad yesterday was, today is a new day. And it's full of new chances to have fun, to do nice things for other people, and to make new friends. Make the most of this wonderful new day!

Thank you for giving me each brand-new day.
Thank you for taking my troubles away.

All Gone

Happy is the person whose sins are forgiven.
Psalm 32:1, ICB

We all make mistakes, and then we usually feel sad! We might hurt someone's feelings, get into trouble, or make our parents angry. But God says he'll forgive our mistakes when we tell him we're sorry. Forgiveness means God takes away our mistakes and acts like they never happened. And that makes us feel *very* happy.

God will forgive me when I make mistakes.
Saying "I'm sorry" is all that it takes.

He's Always Watching

I will instruct you and teach you in the way you should go;
I will guide you with My eye.
Psalm 32:8, NKJV

God is *always* taking care of us. He gave us the Bible to help us know what to do. He always listens to our prayers. He puts people in our lives, like parents and teachers and friends, to help us learn and grow and follow him. That's how God keeps an eye on each of us, every day, forever.

Through family and friends, God shows me the way
To do what he wants me to do every day.

God Loves to Listen

I cried to him and he answered me! He freed me from all my fears.
Psalm 34:4, TLB

Sometimes it's hard to imagine a powerful God taking time to listen to our little problems. But listening to you is one of God's *favourite* things to do. He loves you so much that he can't wait for you to call his name. Whether you're scared or in trouble, God promises that whenever you talk to him, he'll hear you and help you.

I'm never afraid to try something new.
God listens to me, and he helps me, too!

Big Trouble

God is our protection and our strength.
He always helps in times of trouble.
Psalm 46:1, ICB

Have you ever had a really bad day when everything went wrong? The Bible says *everyone* will have problems. But here's the great thing about trouble. When it does come, you're not alone. God is there to help you. And he's stronger and more powerful than any of your troubles. He can help you get through anything!

When trouble comes, I don't have to worry.
God's strength and power make me brave in a hurry.

Always with Me

[God] will be our guide even to the end.
Psalm 48:14, NIV

Have you ever been lost? It's a scary feeling, isn't it? When you get lost, you want someone to point you in the right direction and help you find your way. That's what God does for us. He shows us the right direction to go in life and sticks with us to make sure we never get lost. If we listen to him and pay attention to his directions, we'll always know just where to go.

With you as my guide there is one thing I know.
You always show me which way I should go.

God to the Rescue

I want you to trust me in your times of trouble, so I can rescue you.
Psalm 50:15, TLB

Do you have a dog or a cat in your family? Pets depend on us to feed them and take care of them. If your pet is frightened, you can help it feel safe. And God can help you feel safe too! He rescues you from trouble, just like you would rescue your pet if it was in danger. All you need to do is trust God.

God, you promise to come to my rescue.
When I'm in trouble, I just need to trust you.

Anytime at All

Morning, noon, and night . . . the Lord hears my voice.
Psalm 55:17, NLT

Do you know you can talk to God any time you want? You can say a prayer every night before you go to bed. You can talk to him about your day when you first wake up in the morning. You can thank him for your food at lunch. And you can talk to God anytime in between—when you're playing with your toys, laughing with your friends, or at the park with your dad. Any time is a good time to talk to God!

God's ready to listen when I want to talk.
I can pray when I play, when I run, when I walk.

The Perfect Path

[God] will not permit the godly to slip or fall.
Psalm 55:22, TLB

Going through life is like taking a walk through the woods. There are little twigs that are really easy to step over and big tree trunks you have to climb over. Sometimes you might get lost, and other times you know just where to go. As you walk through life, isn't it nice to know God is walking with you? When you follow his path, you'll never fall or lose your way.

God's path is the best path for one and for all.
If I follow him, then he won't let me fall.

God Is My Hero

I follow close behind you, protected by your strong right arm.
Psalm 63:8, TLB

Do you have a favourite superhero? Superheroes on TV have amazing powers and can do almost anything. But God is even better than a superhero. He protects you and takes care of you in ways you can't even see. He's the most powerful, amazing superhero you could ever want.

God's my hero, great and strong.
Protected by him, I can't go wrong.

In God's Hands

He holds our lives in his hands, and he holds our feet to the path.
Psalm 66:9, TLB

When you hold a little animal in your hands, you have to be very careful. If you squeeze a small animal too tightly, it might get hurt. But if you don't hold on tightly enough, the animal might fall out of your hands and run away. You have to hold it just right. The Bible says God holds our lives in his hands. He takes good care of us, holding us just right.

I'm in God's hands, and he's holding me tight.
He takes care of me each day and each night.

Sunny Days

The Lord God is a sun and shield; . . . no good thing does he withhold
from those whose walk is blameless.
Psalm 84:11, NIV

What would life be like without the sun? Well, it would be very dark, for one thing. But the sun does more than give us light. It keeps us warm and it helps things grow. Everything on earth needs the sun to stay alive. The Bible says God is a sun. Without him, every day would be dark and cold and dreary. But with him, each day is full of light and warmth and happiness.

God gives us light, just like the sun.
Without him, my life would not be as fun.

My Favourite Things

The Lord will indeed give what is good.
Psalm 85:12, NIV

Think about some of your favourite things. Do you like animals? flowers? bugs? apples? your grandma? Where do you think your favourite things came from? That's right, God made them! Every good thing we have—from the people we love to the yummy food we eat—is a gift from God. And God will keep giving us good things forever.

Everything good comes from God up above.
The things that he gives are the signs of his love.

First Aid

In the day of my trouble I will call to you, for you will answer me.
Psalm 86:7, NIV

Ouch! It hurts when you fall down and scrape your knee! You run to your mum, and she gives you a big hug, cleans the scrape, and puts a bandage on it. You stop crying and begin to feel a little better, don't you? Even though scrapes and bruises are no fun, knowing that God will always send you the help you need makes a big difference.

I call out when I fall down.
I know a helper can be found!

Tell Me a Story

I will sing of the tender mercies of the Lord forever!
Young and old will hear of your faithfulness.
Psalm 89:1, NLT

You can learn lots of interesting things from older people—like your grandma, your grandpa, or the nice neighbour down the road. They can show you how to fish, skim stones, or make snow angels. But one of the best things older people can teach you is how to trust God. So the next time you're with people who have lived a long time, ask them to tell you a story about what God has done for them.

Their stories will help you remember that God will always be with you, even when you grow old.

God will be with me as long as I live.
Even when I'm old, I'll have lots to give.

March

Strong and Tall

The righteous will flourish like a palm tree.
Psalm 92:12, NIV

Trees are some of the oldest living things on the earth. Some trees are hundreds of years old! Trees are strong and can grow almost anywhere. They can stand hot sun and cold rain. The Bible says we are like trees. God made us able to stand up to just about anything. With God's help, you can grow tall and strong too, just like the trees.

**I'll grow strong and tall like a tree,
Just the way God made me to be!**

Singing for Joy

Come, let's sing for joy to the Lord.
Psalm 95:1, ICB

When you think about how much God loves you, it's easy to get excited. You just want to sing! You can think of your song as a little prayer. You can tell God how great he is and how glad you are to have him taking care of you. So sing a song and show the whole world the joy of loving God!

When I'm happy, I will sing
About the joy my God can bring!

Forever Friends

The Lord is good. His love continues forever.
Psalm 100:5, ICB

Do you know how long forever is? It's a *lot* longer than a week or a month or a year. Forever is such a long time that it will never, ever end. And that's how long God's love for you will last—forever! That means God will love you long after next week or next month or even next year is over. God will love you longer than you can even imagine.

God's love for me will never end.
Forever God will be my friend.

Sky High

As high as the sky is above the earth, so great is his love
for those who respect him.
Psalm 103:11, ICB

It's a long way up to the sky, isn't it? Can you touch it when
you jump? Can you reach the bird way up there?
Can you see where the sky ends?
No! And God's love is as huge
and amazing as the sky.
And just like the sky,
God's love never,
ever ends.

God's love for me is as big as the sky,
As wide and as clear and as huge and as high.

Long Gone

He has taken our sins away from us as far as the east is from west.
Psalm 103:12, ICB

Sin is a little word with a big meaning. Sins are the wrong things we do that hurt other people, like lying or teasing or disobeying. But when we tell God we're sorry, God takes those things away. In fact, he takes them so far away that even *he* doesn't see them anymore. So when we do something we shouldn't, we can tell God about it, say we're sorry, and know that God will take the wrong we did far, far away.

When I do wrong, what do I say?
"I'm sorry, God," and you take it away.

Free as a Bird

The birds nest beside the streams and sing among
the branches of the trees.
Psalm 104:12, NLT

Have you ever noticed that birds always seem happy? They're always singing. That's because God makes sure the birds have everything they need. He gives them trees to live in, worms to eat, and water to drink. God gives us everything we need too, doesn't he?

I can be happy, like a bird in a tree.
And just like a bird, God takes care of me.

Day by Day

Your strength shall be renewed day by day like morning dew.
Psalm 110:3, TLB

When things in your life are hard, it's easy to get discouraged. Maybe your parents argue sometimes or someone you love is sick. Or maybe your best friend is moving away. But God promises to help you get through all your difficult days. Ask him to help you be strong today.

God will help me all the way.
He gives me new strength day by day.

God's Special Book

[God] is in the heavens. . . .
Psalm 115:3, TLB

God lives in heaven. But he is also alive in his Word, the Bible. The Bible is full of valuable things God wants us to know. And it's full of exciting stories about God and his world. If you want to get to know God, the Bible is a great place to start.

The Bible is God's special book.
When you need answers, take a look.

Never Too Busy

I love the Lord because he hears and answers my prayers.
Psalm 116:1, NLT

It's not fun to talk to someone who isn't really listening. It's frustrating when you want to tell someone a story or ask a question but everyone is too busy to listen. But God is never too busy to listen to you. When you have something to tell him, just say his name. He'll be there, ready to hear you and help you.

God, you know I have lots to say—
Thank you for listening to me today.

Sweet Dreams

I will not be afraid because the Lord is with me.
Psalm 118:6, ICB

When it's time for bed, you might
not always like being alone in your dark
room. But Jesus is with you, even in the dark, even in
the middle of the night. He protects you even when you're
asleep. So you don't have to be afraid of the dark. Just remember
Jesus is watching over you. He'll help you sleep soundly—and
you'll have good dreams.

I am safe when my day ends,
Dreaming dreams that Jesus sends.

Words to Go

I have thought much about your words. I have stored them in my heart.
Psalm 119:11, TSLB

The Bible is full of promises from God. Lots of them are found in the book of Psalms. You've been reading some of them each day in this book. You can learn the ones you like best by heart. Then God's words will be with you all the time!

God's Word is with me wherever I go.
The Bible is full of good things to know.

Lasting Love

Your faithfulness extends to every generation,
as enduring as the earth you created.
Psalm 119:90, NLT

The earth has been around a long time. And since the very beginning, God has loved the people on earth. He loved and cared for your parents when they were small just like you. He watched over your grandparents and your great-grandparents, too! The earth was built to last a long time, and God's faithfulness and love will last even longer!

The love of God will last and last,
Even when this day has passed.

Shine the Light

Your word is a lamp for my feet and a light for my path.
Psalm 119:105, NLT

Taking a walk outside at night can be lots of fun. But you need a torch to help you see where you're going so you won't trip or get lost. The Bible is like a torch. It helps us see where we should go and shows us the right path to take.

God's Word will always light my way.
It tells me what to do and say.

The Greatest Helper

Shall I look to the mountains for help? No!
My help comes from the Lord. He is the one who made the mountains!
And he made the heavens too!
Psalm 121:1, TSLB

God gives you lots of people to love you and help you.
Your parents can help you figure out what to do when you're
confused. The doctor can make you feel better when you're sick.
Your best friend can cheer you up when you're sad. God gave
you parents to love you and doctors to keep
you healthy and friends to make you
laugh. God gives you all the help
you need!

When I need help, who can I call?
I call on God, Creator of all.

Wide Awake

He will never let me stumble, slip, or fall.
For he is always watching, never sleeping.
Psalm 121:3-4, TLB

Your mum and dad do their very best to take care of you. But sometimes you might still get hurt. If you fall down, they want to be there to help you. God loves to help you, too. Just like your parents, God wants you to be safe. But unlike your parents, who can't be awake all the time, God never sleeps. He never takes his eyes off of you.

God watches me each night and day,
When I'm asleep, when I'm at play.

Watching Over You

The Lord himself . . . protects you day and night.
Psalm 121:5-6, TSLB

God is always watching over you. He is never too busy. God, the Creator of the whole world, watches over you himself, 24 hours a day. You never have to be afraid or wonder if God is really around. Whether you're awake or asleep, God is right there with you.

God's not too busy to care for me.
There's nothing I do that he can't see.

Safe in the Storm

The Lord will keep you from all harm—he will watch over your life.
Psalm 121:7, NIV

Have you ever been out in the rain without an umbrella?
You get wet and cold and uncomfortable. Umbrellas are great
for keeping you dry. Well, God is a little like an umbrella. He
shelters you and gives you a safe place to hide from the things
that might hurt you. But unlike an
umbrella, God is always
with you. You don't
have to hunt for
him in your
wardrobe!

When life is hard, God's by my side.
He is always a safe place to hide.

The Best Present

Children are a gift from the Lord.
Psalm 127:3, ICB

What's the best present you've ever been given? A game? A trip to the zoo for your birthday? It's always fun to get gifts, especially ones you really like. Did you know God gave your parents a special gift? *You!* The day you became part of your family is a day your parents will never forget. Ask your parents about the best present *they* ever got. They'll tell you it's you!

God gave my parents a gift, you see.
That wonderful, awesome gift is me!

Thank You!

Give thanks to the Lord because he is good.
Psalm 136:1, ICB

When a friend does something nice for you, it makes you happy. You smile and say, "Thank you!" God does lots of nice things for you too. And he loves it when you say thank you to him. The next time you notice one of the wonderful things God has given you, like a comfy bed or a sunny morning, be sure to say thanks!

I have so much I can thank God for—
My house, my family, my friends, and more.

Food for You

He gives food to every living thing.
Psalm 136:25, TLB

When God created us, he knew we'd need to eat, so he gave us food. Not just any food, but really, really good food. The jam in your sandwich started out as a fruit God helped grow. The milk in your cup came from a cow God created. Chocolate, ice cream, and even pizza are all made from God's good ingredients. God sure is a wonderful chef!

God has given me food to eat—
Fruits and veggies and my favourite treats.

Questions and Answers

When I pray, you answer me and encourage me
by giving me the strength I need.
Psalm 138:3, TLB

Did you ever pray for something to happen and it didn't? When you ask for a baby brother and get a sister instead or pray that your grandpa will get better and he doesn't, you might think God isn't listening. But God really does answer all our prayers. He answers by helping us learn to love the baby he sent us, or by comforting us when someone we love is sick. God might not always give us the answer we want, but he'll always give us the answer we need.

God has answers for all of my prayers.
His answer's a promise to always be there.

The Buddy System

Though I am surrounded by troubles,
you will bring me safely through them.
Psalm 138:7, TLB

Have you ever been doing something and then needed someone to help you? When help arrived, you probably started to feel better right away. Often all we really need is another person to help us out. With a friend to help us, our problem doesn't seem so big anymore. No matter what happens, always remember God promises to send you the help you need.

I'm never alone, so I don't need to fear.
No matter what happens, help is always near.

Big Plans

The Lord will work out his plans for my life.
Psalm 138:8, TLB

It's fun to dream about the future. You can imagine being a ballerina or a movie star or a football player. You don't know what your life will be like when you grow up, but God does. He's given you special gifts and talents to help make the world a better place. Together you and God will have a great future!

Who knows what the future will be?
But God has lots of plans for me.

A Special Creation

You know all about me. . . . You are all around me.
Psalm 139:1, 5, ICB

When you paint a picture, you choose the colours you want and put them where you think they should go. When you make a snowman, you decide where his nose should be. When you make something, you know everything about it. When God made you, he picked out all your parts and put them together. So he knows and loves everything about you. You are his special creation.

God knows me well, inside and out.
He knows what I am all about.

Here, There, and Everywhere

*If I ride the morning winds to the farthest oceans,
even there your hand will guide me.*
Psalm 139:9-10, TLB

The world is full of interesting places to go. Travelling on an aeroplane for the first time is very exciting. So is riding on a train or sailing on a lake! But no matter where you go—on holiday, to your grandparents' house, to another country—God is there with you. In all your adventures, God is by your side.

Wherever I go, whatever I do.
I always know that God's there, too.

Made with Love

*You made all the delicate, inner parts of my body
and knit me together in my mother's womb.*
Psalm 139:13, NLT

You know God loves you. But did you know he loved you even before you were born? God's the one who made you and put you together inside your mum. God's the one who decided what colour your eyes should be and how long your nose should be. God made you very carefully so you'd be just right. And you are!

Dear God, you gave me my hands and my hair.
You made me with love. You made me with care.

Wonderful You

I praise you because you made me in an amazing and wonderful way.
Psalm 139:14, ICB

Do you ever think your feet are too big or your eyes are too green or you have too many freckles? The truth is, God wanted each of us to be unique. He made you exactly the way he thought you should be. When God looks at you, he doesn't see big feet or freckly cheeks. He sees someone he loves, someone he thinks is wonderful!

God made me special, I know it's true.
I am amazing and wonderful, too!

First Things First

*The Lord is faithful to all his promises
and loving toward all he has made.*
Psalm 145:13, NIV

The Bible is full of verses
that remind us of God's
promises and his love for us.
Maybe you've been wondering
why the Bible keeps saying
the same thing over and over
again. It's because the most
important lesson the Bible teaches us
is that God loves us more than we
can imagine. And that's
worth repeating!

The Bible is full of God's words from above.
The best word of all is his wonderful love.

Need a Lift?

The Lord lifts the fallen and those bent beneath their loads.
Psalm 145:14, TLB

Every family goes through tough times. Sometimes someone
we love dies, or there isn't much money for fun things, or mums
and dads have a hard time getting along.
It's during those times that God
promises to lift us up and
keep us going. That doesn't
mean the tough times will
go away in an instant, but
it means you don't have to
go through them alone.

God helps me through good times and bad.
He's even there when I feel sad.

Keep Talking

The Lord is close to all who call on him.
Psalm 145:18, NLT

Even though God is very
powerful, he's not scary to talk to.
You might think only important people
can talk to God, or that you have to use special words or be in
a special place to pray. But God listens to everyone, no matter
who they are or what words they use or where they might be.
So when you need God, just start talking!

Wherever I am, whatever I say,
God's ready to listen to me when I pray.

God Promised!

He is the God who keeps every promise.
Psalm 146:6, TLB

God made lots of promises in the Bible. He promised Noah that he'd never send another flood and then gave Noah a rainbow to help him remember. He promised Abraham and Sarah that they'd have a baby, even though they were older than your grandparents. He promised the Israelites they would always have enough to eat, even when they were living in the desert. And God kept every single one of those promises. When God says he'll do something, he means it.

When God makes a promise, he'll always come through.
He keeps every promise to me and to you.

April

Nice to Hear!

Let everything that lives sing praises to the Lord!
Psalm 150:6, NLT

There's nothing better than having someone say nice things about you. You feel good when your mum tells you you're smart. Or when your teacher says you did a great job learning your numbers. Or when your friend tells you you're funny. God loves to hear nice things, too. So tell him how wonderful he is. Say how much you love him and how thankful you are for all he's done for you!

Saying nice things is so easy to do.
It makes others happy—as well as you!

A Parent's Job

My child, listen to your father's teaching.
And do not forget your mother's advice.
Proverbs 1:8, ICB

Do you know why your mum and dad always tell you what to do and how to do it? Actually, it's their job! God gave you parents to teach you how to take care of yourself. He wants you to be healthy and happy as you grow up. That's why it's important to pay attention to what your parents say and do what they ask.

God gave me parents to help me grow,
To love me and teach me the things I should know.

Everywhere I Look

Behold, I will pour out my spirit on you;
I will make my words known to you.
Proverbs 1:23, NASB

Did you know God is always around, even though you can't see him? Everywhere you look, you can see signs of God's presence. The trees, the flowers, the birds, and the butterflies are all reminders of God's love and the promises he's made. Every time you see something God made, remember that he is with you.

Wherever I look, I can't help but see
God's work in the flowers, the birds, and the trees.

Good Gifts

Never let loyalty and kindness get away from you!
Wear them like a necklace; write them deep within your heart.
Proverbs 3:3, NLT

What are two of the best gifts you can give a friend? Loyalty and kindness. Loyalty means sticking up for your friend, even if other kids make fun of her. It's being friends with someone no matter what. Kindness is thinking about your friend's feelings. It's doing nice things for him, like letting him play with your favourite toy for a while. When you're loyal and kind, you'll never run out of friends!

Help me, God, to be a good friend—
One who is kind and there till the end.

Learning New Things

Trust in the Lord with all your heart;
do not depend on your own understanding.
Proverbs 3:5, NLT

Have you ever wanted to do something but had a hard time figuring it out? Maybe it was learning to tie your shoes. You tried and tried, but you still needed some help. It's hard to do things all by yourself. That's why God wants us to ask for help when we need it. God gave us minds that can learn new things. And we can trust him to surround us with people who can help us figure things out.

God helps me learn things that are new,
From reading a book to tying my shoe!

Wise and Smart

Happy is the person who finds wisdom and gains understanding.
For the profit of wisdom is better than silver,
and her wages are better than gold.
Proverbs 3:13-14, NLT

One of the best parts of growing up is discovering how to do new things. Learning to dress yourself or write your name or read a book is exciting. As you learn, you're getting something the Bible calls *wisdom*. Wisdom means making good choices and following God. So keep learning!

If you want to be wise and smart,
Just follow God with all your heart.

Bedtime Promises

You can lie down without fear and enjoy pleasant dreams.
Proverbs 3:24, NLT

Before you know it,
it's time to get ready for bed! Sometimes it's hard to settle
down and fall asleep. You wish you could play for a little while
longer. You'd like someone to read you just one more story. But
your body needs a full night's sleep so you can have lots of fun
every day. So snuggle under your covers and close your eyes.
And remember that God promises to give you sweet dreams!

God, you are with me when I go to bed,
Putting sweet dreams inside of my head.

Step by Step

For the Lord will be your confidence,
and will keep your foot from being caught.
Proverbs 3:26, NASB

What would you do without your feet? You might not think about them much, but you use them a lot! Your feet help you run fast and jump high. With your feet you can kick a ball, pedal a bicycle, walk up and down big hills, or ride a skateboard. When you try something new, thank God for your two strong feet. And remember, he's with you every step of the way.

God is with you, there's no need to fear.
With each step you take, God will be near.

God Is Awesome

Fear of the Lord is the beginning of wisdom.
Proverbs 9:10, NLT

Why would the Bible say you should "fear" God? After all, God is your very best friend. And you shouldn't be scared of a friend, right? But God is more than a friend. He's the great and powerful Creator of the whole universe! To "fear" God really means you respect him and remember how awesome he is.

God is awesome and powerful, too.
Yet he's a friend to both me and you!

Real Love

Love covers over all wrongs.
Proverbs 10:12, NIV

Have you ever been mad at your mum or dad? You're not the only one! All kids get mad at their parents. But when you love someone, it's hard to stay mad at them for long. Loving others means you forgive them when they make mistakes. It means you're kind to them, even if they're not always kind to you. Most of all, loving others means you care about them the way God cares about you.

When I get angry at those I love,
I can still love them with help from above.

Helping Hands

A person who gives to others will get richer.
Whoever helps others will himself be helped.
Proverbs 11:25, ICB

Can you think of a way to help someone you love? How about helping your little brother get dressed? Or doing the dishes without being asked? You can feed the fish or empty the rubbish bin or rake the leaves. All these are great ways to show love to others. How can you help someone today?

When I help others and do what I should,
It tells them I love them and makes me feel good.

Deep Roots

Only the godly have deep roots.
Proverbs 12:3, NLT

Have you ever seen a tree that's fallen down after a big storm? Strong winds and heavy rain can pull even the biggest tree up by its roots. But trees that have roots deep in the ground are a lot more likely to stay standing, no matter how strong the storm. God wants us to plant our "roots" in him. The more we know about him and the more we trust him, the deeper our roots will go. And those roots will help us stand up in good times and in bad times.

Just like a tree, my roots are strong.
I'll trust in God my whole life long.

You Promised!

God delights in those who keep their promises.
Proverbs 12:22, TLB

It's easy to make a promise, isn't it? Maybe you promised to make your bed or feed the cat. But it's also easy to get busy doing something else and forget to do what you promised. Sometimes it's hard to *keep* a promise! But doing what you say you'll do is a sign that you're growing up. So keep your promises!

I keep my promises every day.
You can count on me to do what I say!

True Riches

Some rich people are poor, and some poor people have great wealth!
Proverbs 13:7, TLB

To some people,
money is very important.
But money can't buy the things that
really make you happy, like friends or fun or love. Of course it's
nice to have money. Then you can buy lots of toys. But having
friends to laugh with and a family that loves you is even better
than toys. If you've got God in your heart and people who love
you, you're the richest kid in town!

**With family and friends and days that are sunny,
I can be rich without any money!**

A Gentle Answer

A gentle answer will calm a person's anger.
But an unkind answer will cause more anger.
Proverbs 15:1, ICB

When someone gets angry with you, it's easy to get angry right back. Before you know it, everyone's yelling or crying. But problems are solved much more quickly if you stay calm. If you talk kindly to others even when you're upset with them (or they're upset with you), you'll be giving a "gentle answer." And God will be pleased with you!

Because I am kind, I will not shout.
I'll try to stay calm and work things out.

Feel Better Fast!

Gentle words cause life and health; griping brings discouragement.
Proverbs 15:4, TLB

How do you feel when you want to play baseball and it starts to rain? Or when you want a hot dog for lunch and there are only hamburgers? Things don't always go the way you want them to. But whining and complaining doesn't help. It makes you feel even worse. So the next time things don't go your way, think about the good parts of your day instead. It won't take long for you to feel better!

Even when things don't go my way,
I can find something good to say.

A Big Smile

Happiness makes a person smile.
Proverbs 15:13, ICB

What do you do when you're happy? Do you laugh? sing? run? jump? hug? giggle? Everyone shows happiness in a different way. But there's one thing we all do. We all smile. When your heart feels happy, a smile just can't help climbing onto your face and hanging around for a while. So sing and giggle and jump and smile. You've got so much to be happy about!

When I am happy, I just have to smile.
And then my smile will stay for a while!

Little Things

Commit to the Lord whatever you do, and your plans will succeed.
Proverbs 16:3, NIV

God cares about everything you do. He's happy when you talk to him and read about him in the Bible. He's pleased when you draw a picture, play with your sister, or pick up your clothes. God is interested in all that you do, from the little things to the big ones. Remember to tell him all your plans!

God, I tell you all my plans.
Big or small, you understand!

Trust and Obey

God blesses those who obey him;
happy the man who puts his trust in the Lord.
Proverbs 16:20, TLB

The Bible says the way to be really happy is to trust God and obey him. When you trust and obey, your heart is full of love. Your mind is full of good thoughts. You want to do kind and helpful things for the people around you. You enjoy every moment of every day. Because you trust God to take care of you, you are happy and blessed!

God takes care of me every day.
I'm happy and blessed when I obey!

Kind Words

Kind words are like honey—sweet to the soul and healthy for the body.
Proverbs 16:24, NLT

Think about how good it feels when someone tells you how wonderful you are. Wouldn't it be nice to make someone else feel that good? Try telling a friend what you like about her. Or tell one of your parents how glad you are that God made you a family. Say thank you to your teacher, tell your grandma you love her, say hello to the new boy next door. A little kindness can make someone's day.

Words of kindness always feel good,
So share them with your neighbourhood!

A Real Friend

A true friend is always loyal.
Proverbs 17:17, TLB

It's fun to play with your friends when everyone is getting along. But what if someone says something mean to someone else? You could join in and be mean too. But a true friend stands up for others, even when they are being teased. It's not always easy to be a loyal friend. But God wants us to be kind and help each other. He'll give you the courage to be a real friend.

When friends of mine are being teased,
I stand up for them and God is pleased.

Be a Blessing

The good person who lives an honest life is a blessing to his children.
Proverbs 20:7, ICB

People come in all shapes, sizes, and colours. God gave everyone different skills and talents, too. That's why our world is such an interesting place. But no matter what you look like or what kind of talents you have, God wants you to be good and live an honest life. If you do, you will always be a blessing to others.

Some people are short, some people are tall,
But those who are good outshine them all!

Do Your Best

The man who tries to be good, loving, and kind finds
life, righteousness, and honor.
Proverbs 21:21, TLB

God knows that no one is perfect. We all make mistakes.
But we can *try* to do our very best
every day. We can ask
God to help us to be
good, loving, and kind.
So you don't have to
worry about being
perfect. God is
happy when
you just do
your best.

Nobody's perfect, and that's okay!
God helps me do my best each day.

God Loves Me

Train a child how to live the right way.
Then even when he is old, he will still live that way.
Proverbs 22:6, ICB

When you were a baby, you couldn't do much of anything except eat and sleep and look cute. And now look at you! You can walk, talk, tell jokes, and sing songs. Your parents helped you learn all these things. They want to teach you as much as they can so you will live the right way. But the most important thing you can learn from your parents is that God loves you very much!

Of all the things I learn as I grow,
God's love for me is the best thing to know!

Word Power

The right word spoken at the right time is as beautiful
as gold apples in a silver bowl.
Proverbs 25:11, ICB

Did you know you have the power to change someone's whole day? That power is inside your mouth! The words you say can change the way another person feels. If someone is sad, a kind word from you can help her feel better. If someone is worried, calm words can help him relax. Think about the words you say. They can make a big difference to someone else!

Help me remember that my words are strong.
They have the power to fix what is wrong.

Friends Are Fun

Never abandon a friend.
Proverbs 27:10, TLB

Friends are special gifts from God. You can never have too many friends! Friends are fun to be with, whether you are going somewhere special or just playing in your garden. They can turn a boring day into a fun adventure. Real friends love each other no matter what. Thank God for a good friend!

Friends are certainly one of God's gifts.
They love you and hug you and give you a lift.

Perfect Timing

There is a right time for everything.
Ecclesiastes 3:1, TSLB

It's not easy to be patient when you want something to happen. Waiting for your birthday to come or for summer to start can be so hard! But God has a time for everything. He made the seasons long enough for flowers and trees to grow. He made the days long enough for both work and play. When you get impatient, remember that everything happens exactly when God wants it to. His time is the perfect time.

God's in control of the days and the seasons.
He plans it all for the greatest of reasons.

Friends for You

If one person falls, the other can help him up.
Ecclesiastes 4:10, ICB

Aren't you glad you have friends? Friends are always willing to help you. A friend can make you feel better when you're sad. A friend can help you up when you fall down and get hurt. God shows you he loves you by giving you good friends. And when you care for your friends, you're showing them God's love too.

I'm glad I have friends to help when I'm sad.
My friends will be with me through good times and bad.

Helping Out

To enjoy your work and accept your lot in life—
that is indeed a gift from God.
Ecclesiastes 5:19, NLT

What chores do you have to do? Set the table? Feed the dog? Clean your room? Chores aren't always fun, but they are an important part of being a family. When everyone helps with the work, there's more time for fun. So do your chores with a smile. You're helping your family and making your house a great place to live!

Working is hard and is not always fun,
But a smile will help you to get the job done.

Wise Words

It is pleasant to listen to wise words.
Ecclesiastes 10:12, TSLB

Adults give children all kinds of instructions: "Stand up straight." "Don't put your elbows on the table." "Eat your vegetables." "Brush your teeth." It's good to follow these instructions because they teach us how to act. The Bible gives us lots of instructions too, like "Love God" and "Love others." The Bible says we will be happy if we listen to these instructions and do what they say.

Wise words make me happy and good.
I listen to them and do what I should.

May

Give with a Smile!

Give generously, for your gifts will return to you later.
Ecclesiastes 11:1, NLT

Sometimes you might not want to share your toys. After all, that means letting someone else have something you want. But when you share, you usually get your toys back. *Giving* something to another person for keeps can be even harder than sharing. But when you give someone a gift, try to give it with a smile. When you do, they'll give a smile right back to you. And a smile is a great gift!

Giving a gift makes me smile.
I feel good for quite a while!

Happy Thoughts

It is a wonderful thing to be alive! . . . Enjoy every minute of it!
Ecclesiastes 11:7, 9, TLB

You can always find something to complain about. But being alive is wonderful! You get to jump in puddles and wrestle with your dad and eat chocolate chip biscuits and enjoy the sunshine. Life is a lot of fun! Instead of complaining about the things that don't seem right, why not thank God? He's the one who gave you this wonderful life full of wonderful people and things.

Thank you, God, for this wonderful day.
I want to enjoy it in every way!

Your Very Own Voice

Shout and sing for joy.
Isaiah 12:6, ICB

God gave you your very own voice. And it doesn't sound like anyone else's! You use your voice for talking. The more words you learn, the more you can talk! But you can also use your voice for singing. When you are happy, singing a song is a good way to show it. God loves to hear your happy voice!

When I feel happy I'll sing a song.
If you're happy too, you can sing along!

No More Tears

The Lord God will wipe away the tears from all faces.
Isaiah 25:8, NRSV

God knows we all feel sad sometimes. But he also promises that one day he'll take all our tears away. Someday, when we get to heaven, we won't feel like crying, we won't get angry, and we won't hurt. Until then, God says he's with us to comfort us and to take the hurt away. Tell him when you feel sad. He's always with you, right by your side.

God will take all of my tears away,
And heaven will be a great place to stay!

Thinking about God

You will keep in perfect peace all who trust in you,
whose thoughts are fixed on you!
Isaiah 26:3, NLT

God wants us to love him and love others. He also wants us to think about him as we go through the day. When you're eating lunch or swinging on the monkey bars or enjoying a day at the beach, think about God. After all, he made you and the world you live in! When you think about him, you'll feel good. And you'll make God happy too.

When I'm at home, when I'm at play,
I think of God all through the day.

Always Learning

The Lord Almighty is a wonderful teacher.
Isaiah 28:29, NLT

It's amazing how much you can learn in just one day. Just today you may have learned how to swim or write your name or button your shirt. And think of all the things God has shown you today! He's shown you how much he loves you by giving you a family. He's shown you how well he takes care of you by helping your parents buy you clothes and food. He's even shown you how much he wants you to have fun by giving you so many activities to enjoy. Imagine what he's got in store for you tomorrow!

I have lots of growing to do,
Learning new things my whole life through.

Quiet Time

In quietness and in confidence shall be your strength.
Isaiah 30:15, KJV

Can you hear someone whisper in a room full of
noise? No! You have to be very still and quiet
to hear a whisper. As powerful as God is,
sometimes he likes to speak to us in a
quiet whisper. That means we need
to take a little time every day to
be still and listen to God. When
we do, we'll hear his words
whispered in our heart.

When I am quiet and still as can be,
God's voice whispers softly to me!

Talking with God

The Lord still waits for you to come to him so he can show you his love and compassion.
Isaiah 30:18, NLT

Life can get pretty busy sometimes. You've got friends to talk to, games to play, and books to read. It can be hard to squeeze in everything you want to do in a day. But God is always waiting for you to come and talk to him. No matter how busy you are, God's always ready to listen and ready to help. So save a few minutes each day to talk with God.

There are books to read and games to play,
But I'll still talk to God today!

God the King

The Lord is our king; it is he who will save us.
Isaiah 33:22, NIV

When you think of a king, what do you think of? Someone who's powerful? Someone you just have to obey? Someone who's in charge of everything and everyone? Well, that's God! He's all those things and more. He's loving and kind. He's ready to forgive our mistakes. He makes sure we have everything we need to be healthy and happy. He's better than any king here on earth. And he's the only king who will be around forever!

Thank you, God, for being my king.
I love you more than anything.

Forever and Ever

The grass dies, and the flowers fall.
But the word of our God will live forever.
Isaiah 40:8, ICB

There are lots of things in the world, like mountains and oceans, that have been around since God created them years and years ago. But even the mountains and oceans will be gone one day. The only thing that will last forever is God's love for us. That's why we put our trust in God. He'll be here even when everything else is gone.

God's love is forever, it will never die.
He will last longer than earth, sea, or sky.

Our Shepherd

He will feed his flock like a shepherd.
He will carry the lambs in his arms, holding them close to his heart.
He will gently lead the mother sheep with their young.
Isaiah 40:11, NLT

God is great and powerful, but he is very gentle, too. He cares for us the way a good shepherd cares for his sheep. If a little lamb gets hurt, the shepherd carries the lamb until it feels better. And when the sheep have babies, the shepherd helps them find a safe place to eat and sleep. The shepherd loves his sheep and does everything he can to care for them. God is our shepherd, and we are his little lambs.

God is my shepherd and I am his lamb.
He keeps me safe wherever I am!

Full of Power

[God] gives power to those who are tired and worn out;
he offers strength to the weak.
Isaiah 40:29, NLT

Our bodies are amazing! Eating food that's good for us, getting lots of exercise, and getting enough sleep are all ways we can help our bodies stay strong and healthy. But even when we take really good care of ourselves, we can still get weak and tired. Working hard can make us feel worn out sometimes! God promises to give extra strength for those times. Just ask him!

When I am tired and feeling weak,
God's strength gives me the help I seek!

Fly like an Eagle

Those who wait on the Lord will find new strength. They will fly high on wings like eagles. They will run and not grow weary. They will walk and not faint.
Isaiah 40:31, NLT

Have you ever seen an eagle? Eagles can fly places other birds can't. They love to fly high in the sky and soar on the wind. The Bible tells us that we can be as strong as an eagle with God's help. We can go places we didn't know we could go and do things we didn't know we could do. When you're having a hard day, ask God to lift you up and make you strong like an eagle.

When I'm discouraged and don't know why,
God gives me strength and helps me to fly.

A Helping Hand

Don't be afraid, because I am your God.
I will make you strong and will help you.
Isaiah 41:10, ICB

It's not always easy being a child. Someone's always telling you you're too young or too little to do the things you want to do. But God helps you grow stronger every day. Not so long ago, you needed help getting dressed, eating lunch, and counting to ten.

Now you may be able to do those things by yourself! The next time someone tells you you're too little to do something, remember that God is helping you get bigger every day.

I may be young, but every day
I grow stronger in some new way.

Always with You

When you go through deep waters and great trouble, I will be with you.
When you go through rivers of difficulty, you will not drown!
Isaiah 43:2, NLT

It would be nice if being part of God's family meant that everything in your life would always be perfect. But everyone has not-so-perfect times. When your life seems less than perfect, remember that God is with you. He promises that no matter how tough or scary life gets, he'll be there. In a not-so-perfect life, it's great to have a perfect friend like God.

God is with me when times are tough,
He comforts me and that's enough.

Promises for a Lifetime

I will be your God throughout your lifetime—until your hair
is white with age. I made you, and I will care for you.
I will carry you along and save you.
Isaiah 46:4, NLT

It might be hard to imagine now, but someday you may be a grandma or a grandpa. What do you think you'll look like then? Will you have gray hair? Or a wrinkly face? You'll change a lot as you grow older, but one thing will never change. God, who loves you so much right now, will keep on loving you every day of your life.

Even when I grow old and gray,
God will still walk with me every day.

My Hiding Place

In the shadow of His hand He has hidden me.
Isaiah 49:2, NKJV

Do you have a favourite place to hide? It's fun to have a secret spot behind a chair or under the bed or out in the garden. You can go there when you want to feel safe or just be by yourself. God is a safe place for us too. His love is like a huge blanket we can wrap ourselves in. We can let God take care of us and keep us safe. When you can't run to your secret place, remember that you can find shelter by praying to God anytime, anyplace.

I have a hiding place no one can see.
God's love will safely and surely hide me.

The Best Love of All

Can a mother forget her nursing child? Can she feel no love for a child she has borne? But even if that were possible, I would not forget you!
Isaiah 49:15, NLT

Have you ever been separated from your mum or dad at the zoo or shops or library? It's scary, isn't it? But it's even scarier for your parents, who love you. Your mum doesn't want anything bad to happen to you. Your dad does everything he can to keep you safe. But as much as they love you, God loves you even more. Just like your parents, God cares about everything you do. And he won't ever let you out of his sight.

God never leaves me out on my own.
He's always with me wherever I roam.

A Shining Light

Feed the hungry and help those in trouble. Then your light will shine out from the darkness, and the darkness around you will be as bright as day.
Isaiah 58:10, NLT

When you were a baby, you needed a lot of help. But the older you get, the more you can help others. If your sister scrapes her knee, you can help put a plaster on it. If a friend doesn't have any lunch, you can share yours. Helping others is a wonderful way to share the light of God's love. How can you help someone today?

I can help if you're in trouble.
I'll be right there on the double!

Just like a Flower

*The Lord will guide you continually, watering your life when
you are dry and keeping you healthy, too. You will be like a
well-watered garden, like an ever-flowing spring.*
Isaiah 58:11, NLT

Spring is a wonderful time of year. Beautiful flowers pop up
everywhere! But flowers can't grow without good soil, lots of
sunshine, and gentle rain. God made flowers—
and the soil, sun, and rain to help
them grow. Like flowers, we
also need the good things
God gives us to help us
grow: good food, warm
clothing, families, and
friends. The next time
you see a flower, think
about what God has
done to help you
grow too.

Just like the flowers that grow from small seeds,
God always gives me the things that I need.

You're Delightful!

The Lord delights in you and will claim you as his own.
Isaiah 62:4, NLT

Of all the things God made, people make him the happiest!
God "delights in you." That means he is full of joy whenever
he thinks of you. Even when you do things you shouldn't, even
when you're in a bad mood, even when you aren't
thinking about him, he's thinking about you. You are
his child, and he thinks you're incredible.

I am God's child and he thinks I'm just right.
He looks at me with great love and delight.

God Always Knows

I will answer them before they even call to me. While they are still talking to me about their needs, I will go ahead and answer their prayers!
Isaiah 65:24, NLT

You don't always know what your mum is planning until she tells you, do you? And you don't always know if someone needs your help unless he asks you. But no matter what's going on in your life right this minute, God already knows about it. If you have a problem, he already knows how to fix it. If you're feeling bad, he's already finding a way to help you feel better. God knows you so well that he takes care of your needs before you even ask him!

Before I call you, God, you're already there.
You know what I need, and I know that you care.

Heavenly Hugs

I will comfort you as a mother comforts her child.
Isaiah 66:13, ICB

Mums and dads are really good at making you feel
better when you're sad. And the Bible says
God is like a parent. He's someone
you can go to whenever you
need a hug or want someone
to listen to you. And just like
your mum or dad always
tries to comfort you, God
keeps you safe and
secure. You can
always turn
to him. He's
glad to help.

My mum and my dad give me lots of love,
And even God gives me hugs from above!

Special Delivery

Before I made you in your mother's womb, I chose you.
Before you were born, I set you apart for a special work.
Jeremiah 1:5, ICB

Have your parents told you about the day you joined their family? About how excited they were when they held you for the very first time? And just think, God knew all about you even before your parents did! Before you took your first breath or cried your first tear, God loved you. He planned a wonderful life for you. And he'll be looking out for you forever.

Before I was born, God knew about me.
He's loved me forever and planned what I'll be.

The Right Path

Ask for the ancient paths, ask where the good way is, and walk in it,
and you will find rest for your souls.
Jeremiah 6:16, NIV

We all make lots of choices during the day.
Some are easy, like deciding which cereal to eat
for breakfast. Others are hard, like deciding
whether to tell your parents the truth
about who broke the lamp. When you
don't know what to do, think about what
God says. He tells us to follow
him and do what's right.
When we do, we can relax
and know we've made the
right choice.

When I must choose between wrong or right,
God will help me to see the light.

On Your Side

Your words made me very happy.
I was happy because I am called by your name.
Jeremiah 15:16, ICB

This verse was written by a man named Jeremiah. He wrote it when he was feeling sad and alone. He had lots of enemies and very few friends. But even when he felt terrible, he remembered that God was on his side. Because he was God's child, he knew God was with him, even during a difficult time. And this made Jeremiah happy. Always remember God is on your side.

I'm happy to know God is always with me.
Close by my side he has promised to be!

Something New

Blessed are those who trust in the Lord and have made
the Lord their hope and confidence.
Jeremiah 17:7, NLT

As long as you live, you'll never run out of new things to learn. You won't be the best at everything, but that should never stop you from trying. Even when you're not quite sure how to do something, you can be sure that God is with you. Even if you don't catch the ball or sing the right note or write the letter A perfectly, God thinks you're great. You may not do everything right, especially the first time. But God loves you just the same.

When I try new things, I might not succeed,
But God's endless love is all that I need.

Your Exciting Future

I know the plans I have for you.
Jeremiah 29:11, NLT

You might not think much about your future, but God's already got big plans for you. You might be a doctor, an artist, or a teacher when you grow up. But whatever you do, God just wants you to follow him. He wants you to share his love with the people you meet as you grow up. He wants you to make good decisions and stay close to him. When you do, you'll be living your life just the way he wants you to.

I want to follow God's wonderful plan.
If I do what he tells me, I know that I can!

Calling on God

When you pray, I will listen.
Jeremiah 29:12, NLT

Prayer is a little bit like talking to your grandma on the telephone. You can't see her, but you know she's there because you can hear her voice. When you pray to God, you can't see him either. You might wonder if he's really there. This verse is God's promise to you that he's always ready to listen. Even though you can't see God, talk to him. Tell him what's going on in your life. He loves to hear from you.

God always listens to me when I pray.
I love to talk with him every day.

Just Look

If you look for me in earnest, you will find me when you seek me.
Jeremiah 29:13, NLT

If you ever wonder where God is, look around you. You can't actually see God. But if you really pay attention, you'll find him. Just look at a butterfly fluttering by and you'll see God's amazing creativity. Or listen to a rainstorm and you'll hear God's power. Feel a warm hug from someone you love and you'll feel God's love, too. God really is right here with us. All we have to do is look.

God's love surrounds me in flowers and trees,
In people and rainstorms, in bullfrogs and bees!

God's Promise

You will be my people, and I will be your God.
Jeremiah 30:22, NIV

Long ago, God made a special promise that can never be broken. He said we will always be his people and he will always be our God. All through the Bible, people did things they shouldn't, but God still loved them. We all make mistakes every day, but God still loves us. God has kept his promise since the beginning of time. We will be God's people and he will be our kind, loving God forever and ever. That's a promise!

God made a promise he never will break.
He'll love us forever, whatever it takes.

June

Everlasting Love

I have loved you with an everlasting love.
Jeremiah 31:3, NASB

Who do you love most? Your parents? Your favourite cuddly toy? Your puppy? When you really love someone, it doesn't matter if they hurt your feelings sometimes or make mistakes. You love them anyway. That's how God feels about you. His love for you is so strong that it will last forever. He'll love you when you hurt his feelings. He'll love you when you make mistakes. He'll love you every day of your life!

God's love for me will never end.
I'm so glad that he's my friend.

God Is Near

*I will turn their mourning into joy. I will comfort them
and exchange their sorrow for rejoicing.*
Jeremiah 31:13, NLT

Everyone goes through difficult times once in a while. But God tells us that these difficult times won't last for long. If your family is going through a hard time, remember that God is with you and will comfort you. And remember that someday soon, God will bring joy back to your family. The bad times won't last forever, but God's love and care always will.

Some days are fun, and some days are not.
On all kinds of days, God loves me a lot!

Nap Time

I will refresh the weary and satisfy the faint.
Jeremiah 31:25, NIV

When you're really sleepy, nothing feels better than a nice little nap. Taking a rest in the middle of a busy day can make you feel so much better. Spending time with God can be like a little nap for your heart. Whether you're talking with God or just enjoying the world he made, your heart gets filled up with God's love. You're full of energy again!

Taking a nap gives me a fresh start.
Talking with God is a nap for my heart!

Blue Skies

You have made the heavens and earth by your great power;
nothing is too hard for you!
Jeremiah 32:17, TLB

On a warm summer day, isn't it nice to be outside with your friends? It's fun to lie in the grass and look up at the blue sky and fluffy white clouds. Isn't it amazing to think about God creating such a beautiful world? Only God could be powerful enough to make the sun and the wide-open sky. And you get to enjoy it all!

God, how did you make the sky so blue?
You're so powerful and wonderful, too!

Just Ask

Call to Me, and I will answer you.
Jeremiah 33:3, NASB

When you're hungry, people give you food, don't they? When you're tired, they probably help you find a cosy place to sleep. Whenever you need something, you can ask someone who cares about you for help. They'll give it to you! That's how God is too. No one cares about you more than he does! When we need his help with a big or small problem, all we have to do is ask.

God will help you—just give him a call!
He takes care of problems, the big and the small.

Power When You Need It

The one who redeems them is strong. His name is the Lord Almighty.
Jeremiah 50:34, NLT

When you're young, you don't have much control over what happens to you. Your parents decide what you should wear, what you should eat, and where you should go. Older kids might say you can't play with them because you're not strong enough to throw the ball or a fast enough runner. But even when you're young, you have God on your side. You might not have much power on your own, but God's got enough for both of you!

I might be young and not very strong,
But God will be with me my whole life long!

Lots of Love

The Lord's love never ends. His mercies never stop.
Lamentations 3:22, ICB

When you get in trouble, you might think your parents don't love you anymore. But even when they're upset with you, your mum and dad love you more than you can imagine. The same is true of God. Even when you do things you shouldn't, God loves you. He'll forgive you when you ask him. And he'll never stop loving you.

God's love for me goes on and on.
He even loves me when I do wrong.

Brand-New Day

His love and kindness begin fresh each day.
Lamentations 3:23, TSLB

Every day is a brand-new beginning! The sun wakes up and you wake up, too. You're happy and raring to go. Just think of all the fun things you might do! You might fly a kite in the park, take your dog for a walk, or go for a swim. Each new day is one to enjoy.

God's love for me is fresh every day.
He loves to show me in all kinds of ways!

A New Friend

The Lord is wonderfully good to those who wait for him and seek him.
Lamentations 3:25, NLT

If you want to make new friends, you have to do a little work. You have to talk to people, ask them about themselves, and spend time with them. Getting to know God takes a little work too. To really grow close to God, we need to talk to him often, find out more about him by reading the Bible, and make him part of each day. When we do, he'll be our friend forever!

God, you are my very best friend.
You'll be my friend until the end.

The Holy Spirit

I will put my Spirit in you and you will live.
Ezekiel 37:14, NIV

Since God can't be here on earth with us, he gave us a special gift called the Holy Spirit. The Holy Spirit helps us make good decisions and helps us follow God. Most of all, the Holy Spirit lives in our hearts and helps us remember how much God loves us. What a wonderful gift!

The Holy Spirit is special to me—
God's love is what he helps me see.

Beautiful Things

How great are his signs, how powerful his wonders!
Daniel 4:3, NLT

Everything God made—from raindrops and butterflies to children like you—tells us something about God. Raindrops help things grow and show us that God takes good care of the things he made. Butterflies show us that God has fun making beautiful things for us to enjoy. You are a reminder that God loves to bring new people into the world. Look around you. What else can you learn about God?

From birds that fly to fish that swim,
All God made points me to him.

The Eternal King

He is the living God and he endures forever;
his kingdom will not be destroyed,
his dominion will never end.
Daniel 6:26, NIV

The Bible was written thousands of years ago. Back then, Daniel, the man who wrote this verse, had no idea that you would someday read his story to learn about God. But Daniel knew one thing for sure. He believed God would still be in control, even in the future. And he was right. The God who helped Daniel is the same God who helps you today.

God's love lasts for all generations.
He's the King of people and nations.

Forgive and Forget

The Lord our God is merciful and forgiving.
Daniel 9:9, NIV

Have you ever had to forgive someone? It's not easy, is it? When your sister hurts your feelings or ruins something that belongs to you, it can really make you angry. But when she says she's sorry and asks to be forgiven, you need to do your best to forgive her. Remember, God forgives us every time we ask him to. And when we forgive each other, it feels so much better!

I can forgive when someone hurts me.
I know that's the way God wants me to be!

A Sure Thing

Oh, that we might know the Lord! Let us press on to know him!
Then he will respond to us as surely as the arrival of dawn
or the coming of rains in early spring.
Hosea 6:3, NLT

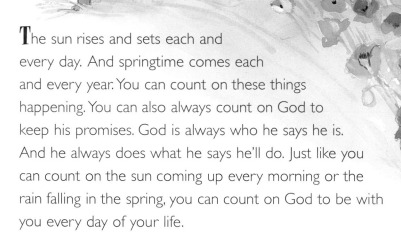

The sun rises and sets each and
every day. And springtime comes each
and every year. You can count on these things
happening. You can also always count on God to
keep his promises. God is always who he says he is.
And he always does what he says he'll do. Just like you
can count on the sun coming up every morning or the
rain falling in the spring, you can count on God to be with
you every day of your life.

Just like the sun comes up each day,
I know God is with me all the way.

God Is Perfect

No, I will not punish you as much as I really should. . . .
For I am God and not man.
Hosea 11:9, TSLB

We don't know everything about God, but we do know that God is very different from people. People make mistakes, but God is perfect. People can be mean, but God is always kind. People get mad at each other, but God always forgives us. People sometimes hate one another, but God loves us forever. Aren't you glad we've got a God like that?

God is perfect and loving and good.
The way that he acts is the way that we should!

The Tree of Life

I am the one who looks after you and cares for you. I am like a tree that is always green, giving my fruit to you all through the year.
Hosea 14:8, NLT

What does an apple tree look like? Is it full of green leaves—and sometimes apples? This verse says that God is like a tree. And even better, unlike real trees, he produces fruit all year round! That means God gives us everything we need, every time we need it. An apple tree doesn't have any apples on it during the winter. But God's love and care never end.

**God takes care of my needs every day.
Beside me I know he always will stay.**

Follow God

The ways of the Lord are right; the righteous walk in them.
Hosea 14:9, NIV

As you get older, people may try to make you do things you know aren't right. Someone might tell you it's okay to lie or take something that doesn't belong to you. Other people might tell you that God's rules are too hard to follow or that they don't matter. But those people are wrong. The rules God gives us are there to protect us. When we obey God's rules, we're following the right leader.

God, your rules are all that I need.
I want to follow wherever you lead.

Let It Rain

*Rejoice in the Lord your God! For the rains he sends are
an expression of his grace.*
Joel 2:23, NLT

You might not think of
rain as a gift from God,
especially when you
want to play outside.
But rain is a gift we
can't live without.
If it never rained, we
wouldn't have apples
or strawberries or
oranges. We wouldn't
have milk to drink
(cows need to eat grass to make milk). We wouldn't
have bread to eat (it's made out of wheat that grows on farms).
We wouldn't even have clothes to wear (clothes are sometimes
made from cotton, which grows in fields). Now aren't you glad
God gave us the gift of rain?

**Whenever the rain falls out of the sky,
I thank you, God, for now I know why.**

Forever with God

Everyone who calls on the name of the Lord will be saved.
Joel 2:32, NIV

Sometimes people think that following God is a lot of work. They think you have to do and say all the right things and live a perfect life to get to heaven. But God says all we need to do to live with him forever is ask him to be with us. When we trust God to care for us, we are telling him that we love him—and that we want him to be the most important part of our life. So follow God. It's easy!

**Spending forever with God is no task.
If I want him to save me, I just need to ask.**

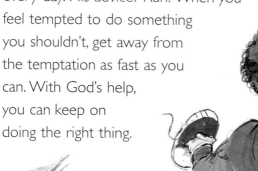

Run Away!

Do what is good and run from evil—that you may live!
Amos 5:14, NLT

Do you know what *temptation* is? It's wanting to do something you know you shouldn't, like taking the last sweet when you told your sister she could have it. God knows we face temptation every day. His advice? Run! When you feel tempted to do something you shouldn't, get away from the temptation as fast as you can. With God's help, you can keep on doing the right thing.

When I face temptation, I just run away.
God always helps me to follow his way.

A Whale of a Tale

I cried out to the Lord in my great trouble, and he answered me.
Jonah 2:2, NLT

Jonah was a man who got himself into big trouble. When Jonah didn't obey God, he ended up caught in a storm while he was out on a boat. Even worse, he was thrown overboard and swallowed by a huge fish! But even after all that, Jonah knew he could trust God to help him. He asked God to take care of him, and God did. He got Jonah out of the fish and kept him safe. If God can take care of Jonah, he can take care of you, too.

When I'm in trouble, God knows what to do.
He rescued Jonah. He'll rescue me, too!

Finding Your Way

The Lord himself will guide you.
Micah 2:13, NLT

You've been hearing a lot about following God and living the way he wants you to. If you're not sure how to do that, don't worry. Let God help you. Read the Bible, talk to him, and listen for his voice in your heart. God will never leave you on your own. He'll be right beside you every day, helping you find your way.

Whenever I struggle to find my way,
God makes sure that I don't stray.

Growing Up

We will walk in the name of the Lord
our God for ever and ever.
Micah 4:5, NIV

As you grow up, lots of things about you will change. You'll look different, you'll live in a different house, and you might even have a different last name someday. But no matter how much you change, one thing will always stay the same. God will always be with you. Even when you go off to college or get married or become a grandparent, God will be there watching out for you and taking care of you.

No matter how much I will change as I grow,
God will stay with me forever—I know!

Help at Hand

As for me, I look to the Lord for his help.
Micah 7:7, NLT

When you need help, you can find it in lots of places. Your parents can help you, and your friends, and your teacher, too. But there will be times when it seems there's no one around to help. That's why it's so important to have God in your life. He's with you all the time. He can help whenever you need him.

I can get help from the people I know,
And God's also with me wherever I go.

Night and Day

*God will bring me out of my darkness
into the light, and I will see his goodness.*
Micah 7:9, TLB

When you're sick with a
cold, it can seem like it will
never end. Or when you wake
up scared in the middle of the
night, you might wonder if the
sun will ever come up. But just like
the night always turns into day, bad times
eventually turn into good times. If you're
having a hard time right now, ask God to
help you get through it. He'll comfort you
until you feel sunny again!

Just as the sun takes the place of the moon,
I know that good days will come again soon.

A Good Place

The Lord is good, a refuge in times of trouble.
He cares for those who trust in him.
Nahum 1:7, NIV

Doesn't it feel good to cuddle with your mum? Or curl up on your bed with your favourite cuddly toy? Don't you love holding your dad's hand when you're out for a walk? Whatever you do, make sure you turn to God, too. God promises to always be your refuge—a safe place.

God will help me feel safe and warm,
He shelters me from all kinds of harm.

A Starry Sky

I stand in awe of your deeds, O Lord.
Habakkuk 3:2, NIV

The night sky is really amazing. It's full of sparkling stars, zooming meteors, and of course the big, bright moon. And God is the one who formed all those zillions of stars and all the planets. He made the meteors and the moon. As you look up at the deep, dark sky tonight, say a prayer. Thank God for his wonderful creation. It's his gift to you.

The stars in the sky twinkle brightly each night,
Reminding me of God's deep love and delight.

Climbing High

The sovereign Lord is my strength! He will make me as surefooted as a deer and bring me safely over the mountains.
Habakkuk 3:19, NLT

Have you ever seen a deer running in a field? Deer can run quickly and easily over fields and even mountains. When you have a hard day, it's like a mountain that's tough to climb over. This verse says God will help us climb the "mountains" that show up in our lives. With God at our side, we can be as graceful as deer!

No mountain of trouble is too high for me.
God helps me run like a deer, you see!

Love Songs

[The Lord] will take great delight in you . . .
he will rejoice over you with singing.
Zephaniah 3:17, NIV

God loves it when you sing a song to him. But did you know that God sings to you, too? God loves you so much that sometimes he can't help but sing a song to you! His song might sound like birds twittering in the trees or a gentle breeze blowing through the leaves. It might sound like rain or a waterfall or crickets chirping at night. Each sound is a love song straight from God's heart to you.

I hear God singing to me everywhere,
From the trees to the lake to the peaceful night air.

Wherever You Go

I will make my people strong with power from me!
They will go wherever they wish, and wherever they go
they will be under my personal care.
Zechariah 10:12, TLB

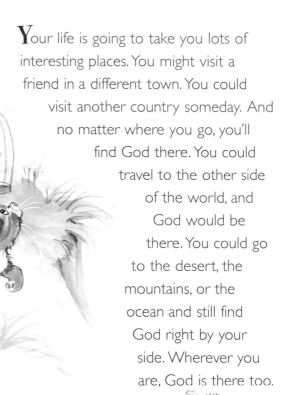

Your life is going to take you lots of interesting places. You might visit a friend in a different town. You could visit another country someday. And no matter where you go, you'll find God there. You could travel to the other side of the world, and God would be there. You could go to the desert, the mountains, or the ocean and still find God right by your side. Wherever you are, God is there too.

Alone in the desert or out on the sea,
God will be there, always caring for me.

July

Since the Very Beginning

I am the Lord—I do not change.
Malachi 3:6, TLB

When you hear exciting stories from the Bible, maybe you wonder if God still watches over people the way he did all those years ago. The answer is yes! Just like God helped Noah escape the Great Flood and helped Jonah survive in the belly of a big fish, God protects you today. Just like he forgave King David for his mistakes and stayed with the people of Israel even when they turned their backs on God, God forgives you today. God has loved and cared for his people since the beginning of time. And he will love and care for you forever!

God is the same, yesterday and tomorrow.
He's always with us in joy and in sorrow.

Don't Wait!

Change your hearts and lives because the kingdom
of heaven is coming soon.
Matthew 3:2, ICB

When you meet a new friend you really like, it would be silly to say, "I don't want to be friends now. Let's wait until we're older." If you did, you'd miss out on some great times! The same thing is true with God. Sometimes people think they don't need to spend time with God until they're older. But if we wait to be friends with God, we'll miss out—on his special love, his help, and his friendship. So don't wait—be God's friend today!

I don't have to wait to be God's friend,
And friendship with God will never end!

JULY 3

Look on the Bright Side

Those who are sad now are happy. God will comfort them.
Matthew 5:4, ICB

Everyone feels sad at times. But God loves us so much that he always finds ways to make us feel better. Our parents hug us and wipe away our tears. Our friends make us laugh and play with us when we're lonely. The sunshine chases away gloomy clouds. The next time you feel sad, look on the bright side. What's making you feel happy again?

If things look gloomy from your point of view,
Remember to look on the bright side too!

Doing What's Right

Those who want to do right more than anything else are happy.
God will fully satisfy them.
Matthew 5:6, ICB

What would you do if a friend
told you to do something wrong?
Doing what's right isn't
always easy. People
might make fun of
you or tell you
you're weird. But
when you do the
right thing, you're also
doing the best thing.
Doing what's wrong leads to
trouble. Doing what's right will always
make you happy in the end. You feel good
when you know you're doing what God wants
you to do.

It feels so good to do what is right—
To follow God with all of your might.

A Pure Heart

Blessed are the pure in heart, for they will see God.
Matthew 5:8, NIV

The Bible says that you will be happy if you have a pure heart. Having a pure heart means you see the good in other people and events. For instance, if it's a rainy day, a person with a pure heart knows that God sent the rain to help the flowers grow. If a friend is in a bad mood, a person with a pure heart sees past her friend's crabbiness to the sadness he might be feeling. Ask God to give you the blessing of a pure heart.

With a heart that's pure, I can see
All the goodness surrounding me!

The Greatest Prize of All

Rejoice and be glad. You have a great reward waiting for you in heaven.
Matthew 5:12, ICB

If someone asked you to describe heaven, what would you say? Do you think it's a place filled with angels, fluffy white clouds, and streets of gold? The Bible doesn't tell us exactly what heaven will look like. But it does say that those who believe in Jesus will live there forever with God. Even when life is tough, we can look forward to the greatest prize of all—heaven!

Life here on earth is just the beginning.
Heaven's the prize we can all be winning!

Love for Everyone

I tell you, love your enemies. Pray for those who hurt you.
Matthew 5:44, ICB

Of all the things God asks us to do, loving an enemy is one of the hardest. How can you love a person you don't even like? How can you pray for someone who hurts you? That's where God comes in. Ask him to give you extra love in your heart. Then you can be kind to people who aren't kind to you. Who knows—you might even become friends!

Although loving others can sometimes be tough,
God fills me with love that's more than enough.

Beautiful Flowers

*If God cares so wonderfully for the flowers that are here today
and gone tomorrow, won't he more surely care for you?*
Matthew 6:30, NLT

Summer is the time for flowers! The next time you're riding in a car, try to notice all the beautiful wildflowers growing on the side of the road or in the fields. Those plants don't belong to anyone, so it's up to God to help them grow. How? He makes sure they have all the rain and sunshine they need. And God cares for you, too—even more than he cares for the plants. When you see beautiful flowers, remember how God cares for them— and for you, too!

God, you care for all the flowers I see.
You help them grow, just like you help me!

From Day to Day

[God] will give you all you need from day to day if you live for him.
Matthew 6:33, NLT

God promises to give you what you need from day to day. Maybe you don't have as many toys as you'd like. Maybe some of your friends seem to have a lot more than you do. Even if you like the toys you have, there always seems to be some new toy that you  think you need. But God wants you to be content with what you have. You might not always get everything you *want,* but you can be sure you'll always have what you *need.*

God, you give me all that I need.
Your love for me is guaranteed!

One Day at a Time

Don't worry about tomorrow. . . . Tomorrow will have its own worries.
Matthew 6:34, ICB

Life is meant to be lived one day at a time. But it's easy for people—especially grown-ups!—to forget this. Instead of enjoying today, they're already worrying about what they'll do tomorrow. But today is full of wonderful moments, and God wants us to enjoy each day fully. So don't worry about tomorrow. Enjoy today!

Today is so full of good things to see,
That tomorrow can just wait for me.

Hidden Treasure

Everyone who continues asking will receive.
He who continues searching will find. And he who
continues knocking will have the door opened for him.
Matthew 7:8, ICB

Pretend you are going on a treasure hunt. You have a map and a list of clues to help you search. You're all excited, but then you have a hard time finding the treasure. Does that make you want to quit? Maybe. But the Bible says that if you keep searching, you'll find what you're looking for in the end. So whether you're looking for buried treasure or trying to find answers to questions you have about God, never give up!

 If you don't give up, you'll find it's true
The answers you need will come to you.

Good Things

Surely your heavenly Father will give good things to those who ask him.
Matthew 7:11, ICB

When you ask your mum and dad for something good, they will do everything they can to make sure you get it. If you tell them you're cold, they'll give you a warm blanket. When you're hungry, they'll make sure you have enough to eat. God is a lot like your parents. He loves to give you good things when you ask for them. You never have to be afraid of asking God for the good things you need.

I talk to God, and he hears what I say.
He meets all my needs each minute, each day.

Live and Love

Do for other people the same things you want them to do for you.
Matthew 7:12, ICB

How does God want you to live? Just remember this verse. God wants you to treat others the way you'd like to be treated. When you see someone who needs help, give him a hand. When someone talks to you, listen to what she says. Give hugs, be kind, and show people the kind of love you like to be shown.

If my friend needs some help and I happen to see,
I'll help him the way I'd want him to help me.

Solid Ground

Anyone who listens to my teaching and obeys me is wise,
like a person who builds a house on solid rock.
Matthew 7:24, NLT

Have you ever built a sand castle? They're fun to build, aren't they? They look great, but they don't really last very long. A good, strong wave will knock them over. If you want to build something that lasts, you need to use stronger materials than sand. God says we should build our lives on something strong too—his teaching in the Bible. Listening to God is just like building a house on solid rock instead of shifting sand.

When I listen to God, I'm on solid ground.
I'll be wise no matter what comes around.

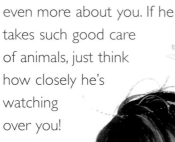

You're Worth It!

Don't be afraid. You are worth much more than many birds.
Matthew 10:31, ICB

God always takes good care of his creation. He makes sure all the animals have places to live. And when an animal gets hurt, God knows about it. He even notices when a little bird falls out of its nest or a bunny needs food. But the Bible says he cares even more about you. If he takes such good care of animals, just think how closely he's watching over you!

God cares for the squirrels and birds that I see.
But I know he cares even more about me!

A Light Load

For My yoke is easy, and My load is light.
Matthew 11:30, NASB

When you're young and your legs are short, you get tired out more quickly than someone taller does. Just when you think you can't walk another step, someone picks you up and carries you. Aren't you glad? Someone bigger and stronger than you doesn't think you are heavy at all. God is the biggest, strongest person in the universe. And he wants us to turn over all our worries and cares to him. Our worries are too heavy for us, but they are a light load for God!

God knows my worries are too heavy for me.
He'll carry them all so that I can be free.

Like a Child

Whoever humbles himself like this child is the greatest
in the kingdom of heaven.
Matthew 18:4, NIV

Lots of kids can't wait to be older. They want to be taller or smarter or stronger so they can do all the things grown-ups do. But God says grown-ups should be more like kids! Children are usually more trusting. They believe God will take care of all their needs. They know God is with them. But sometimes grown-ups forget those things. As you grow up, don't forget all the lessons you've learned about God. There's nothing childish about trusting him.

As small and young as I might be,
It's true that grown-ups can learn from me!

JULY 18

Time with God

Where two or three gather together because they are mine,
I will be right there among them.
Matthew 18:20 TLB

Do you know why people
go to church? A big
reason is that it's a
place where we can
be with God. But
there are many
other places to enjoy
God's presence too. When
you and your family pray before
dinner, God is there. When you play
outside with a friend in the world God
created, God is there. When you sing
a song about God or thank him
for all the great things he's given
you, God is there. So when you
want to spend time with God, grab a friend.
Then invite God to join you!

I can spend time with God anywhere.
Whatever I do, he'll always be there.

Love Yourself!

Love your neighbour as you love yourself.
Matthew 19:19, ICB

God wants you to love everyone. But before you can really love someone else, you have to love yourself! You are a very special person, and God loves you very much. And he wants you to believe it! When you do, you'll begin to see other people differently. The friend you play with, the person who delivers your mail, the teenager who baby-sits for you—you know they are all special people created and loved by God. You can love others and love yourself, too!

God, I am special and loved by you.
I love other people—they're special too!

Do the Impossible!

With God, everything is possible.
Matthew 19:26, TLB

Can God help you do
something really big? Sure he can!
After all, who made the stars and the moon? Who made the
sun and the rain? Who made you and every other person? If
God can do all that, he can help you with anything. Maybe you
think you can't possibly learn to swim, or ride a bike, or learn to
read all by yourself. But don't forget who's on your side. You can
do much more than you think!

When I have the power of God on my side,
I can do things I haven't yet tried!

Believe It!

Whatever things you ask in prayer, believing, you will receive.
Matthew 21:22, NKJV

When you ask God for something, what do you think he does? Does he forget about you? Does he wait to see if you deserve what you've asked for? No. When you ask God for something, he hears you. Best of all, he promises to answer. When you pray, ask God for the things you really need. Then trust him to give you what you ask for—even in unexpected ways!

When I talk to God, he listens and cares.
I can trust God to answer my prayers.

Small Things

You have been faithful in handling this small amount,
so now I will give you many more responsibilities.
Matthew 25:21, NLT

Jesus told his friends a story about a man who went on a long trip. Before he left, he gave each of his servants a different job to do. Some jobs were big and some were small. When he returned, he was very pleased with the servant who did his small job well. Because of this, the man gave the servant a more important job. Remember this story when your parents give you jobs to do. When you do even small jobs well, your parents will be able to trust you more. Maybe they'll say you can ride your bike down the road or stay overnight with a friend!

I'll show my parents that they can trust me.
I'll do all I'm asked, and then they will see.

Do It for Jesus

*I tell you the truth. Anything you did for any
of my people here, you also did for me.*
Matthew 25:40, ICB

Jesus is God's Son. When he lived
on earth, he showed people
how to follow God.
One of the things
he taught is that
we need to treat
everyone the way
we would treat
him. If you saw
Jesus sitting alone
at a playground,
you'd go and talk to him. If you
saw that Jesus was sad or scared or hurt, you'd try to help him.
Jesus said we need to do the same for the people around us.
Whenever we show love to one of God's people, we're
showing love to God, too.

When I help a person who's scared or feels blue,
It's just like I'm helping Jesus, too.

You Can Be Sure

[Jesus said,] "You can be sure that I will be with you always."
Matthew 28:20, ICB

When Jesus left the earth to go to live in heaven with God, his Father, he made a promise to all his friends on earth. He said he'd be with them forever. And that's not the first time that kind of promise was made. God made the same promise to us at the beginning of the Bible, before Jesus came to live on earth. Why did God give us that promise twice? To make sure we know that God, our Father, and Jesus, his Son, are always with us. Together they, along with God's Spirit, protect us, answer our prayers, forgive our mistakes when we say we are sorry, and show us their love.

To know God is with me is always nice.
The Bible says so not once, but twice!

Going Fishing

Come, follow me! And I will make you fishermen for the souls of men!
Mark 1:17, *TLB*

If you've ever gone fishing, you know you need bait—something the fish want—to catch anything. The same is true for telling people about God. When we share God's love with others, they'll feel so good that they'll want to know more about him. You don't have to do anything special to tell people about God. Just love them and care about them. And before you know it, they'll be hooked!

**When you look at my life, I hope you will see
The love of God shining brightly through me.**

A Doctor's Touch

Healthy people don't need a doctor—sick people do. I have come to call sinners, not those who think they are already good enough.
Mark 2:17, NLT

How do you feel when you have a sore throat and a fever? Bad, right? When you're sick, you—and your parents!—are glad your doctor knows just the right medicine to make you feel better. Jesus tells us that, just like a doctor, he came to help those who need him. When you're sick, you need a doctor. And when you realise you need help, Jesus is right there to forgive you and help you.

**Medicine might make you feel good as new,
But Jesus is the one forgiving you!**

Listen and Learn

To those who are open to my teaching,
more understanding will be given.
Mark 4:25, NLT

Listening is a very important thing to do. But it isn't always easy. Sometimes your mum or dad might say, "Share your toys" when you don't feel like sharing. Or they might say, "Tell the truth" when you've just made a mistake. But God says it's important to listen. Your parents can help you learn how to follow God better. So when they speak, it's good to listen—and understand.

Parents can teach you what's right and what's wrong.
They'll help you learn how to get along.

For His Sake

*If you give up your life for my sake and for the sake
of the Good News, you will find true life.*
Mark 8:35, NLT

As you grow up you will discover you can do many things. You
may find out that you can write stories. Or paint pictures. Or
sing beautifully. And you'll want to use your talents to become
all you can be. But always
remember that your
talents are gifts from
God. He wants you
to use them to spread
his love to his world.
What talents do you
have that you can share
with others today?

Whatever my gifts, they're all from God's hand.
Sharing his love through them will be so grand!

Good Deeds

*If anyone gives you even a cup of water because you belong to the
Messiah, I assure you, that person will be rewarded.*
Mark 9:41, NLT

Even though you are very young, you can make a big difference in the lives of those around you. When your mum is tired, give her a hug. When your sister is sad, sing her a song. When a friend needs a playmate, invite him to your house. Being kind to others pleases God. And it means a lot to the people you care about.

**Caring and sharing is how you should live.
Try it and see just how much you can give!**

Important to Jesus

Let the little children come to me. Don't stop them.
Mark 10:14, ICB

One day when Jesus lived on earth some mums and dads brought their little children to Jesus so he could bless them. But some adults thought the kids shouldn't bother Jesus. These adults tried to send the kids away. But how wrong the adults were! Jesus told them plainly that children like you are important to him. Why? Because you show grown-ups how to love and trust God. Why not give that wonderful gift to the adults around you?

Jesus loves little children like me.
Trusting and loving is the way to be!

Who's First?

Many who are first will be last, and the last first.
Mark 10:31, NKJV

Being important
makes some
people feel
special. They'll
hurt people's
feelings or cheat
or lie to make sure
they're first at everything.
But God's incredible love turns
all the world's rules upside down.
The people who stand out to God are often
not the ones who are well known here on earth. Instead, they
are people who quietly love God more than anything else. They
care about others and are kind and thoughtful. Even if you do
become famous when you grow up, always remember what
God thinks is important. Try to be that kind of person first.

If you think you must be first in line,
Know that God's view is different at times.

August

A Special Baby

[The] Holy One who is to be born will be called the Son of God.
Luke 1:35, NKJV

You've already heard about some of the special things Jesus did and said when he lived on earth. But Jesus was special even before he was born. Jesus' mother, Mary, found out she was going to have a baby when an angel arrived at her house and told her. How exciting! The angel also told Mary that her baby would be God's own Son. Now *that's* a pretty special baby!

The angel had something special to say.
God's very own Son was on the way!

True Faith

You are blessed because you believed what the
Lord said to you would really happen.
Luke 1:45, ICB

The angel who visited Mary told her that
she was to be the mother of God's
own Son. Mary got this news
months before Jesus was
ready to be born. And
even though the angel's
news was hard to believe,
Mary trusted God. She
waited patiently. Finally Jesus
was born, and Mary was
happy because she
believed God's promise.

Mary believed the angel's great news.
Trusting God is the best thing to choose.

The Shepherds' Surprise

Shepherds were in the fields. . . . [An] angel said to them, "Don't be afraid,
because I am bringing you some good news. It will be a joy to
all the people. Today your Saviour was born."
Luke 2:8, 10-11, ICB

Can you imagine what those shepherds must have felt like? They were out late at night watching their sheep. They were probably tired and cold and maybe a little bored. Then, out of nowhere, an angel showed up! He gave them the most incredible news in history. God's Son, Jesus, had been born! Sometimes we forget just how amazing it is that God cared enough about us to send his only Son to live on earth with us. But he did. And that's really something to celebrate!

Good news came to them while they watched their sheep.
God's Son was born when most folks were asleep.

Full of Questions

Jesus was sitting . . . with the religious teachers. . . . All who heard him were
amazed at his understanding and wise answers.
Luke 2:46-47, ICB

When Jesus was a little boy, he probably liked a lot of the same things you do, like laughing and playing games with friends. He also liked to learn, especially about the things his heavenly Father was doing in the world. So he talked to God and to people who knew the answers, like teachers and his parents. When you want to know more about God, do what Jesus did. Talk to the grown-ups in your life. Ask lots of questions!

God, there's so much I can know about you.
If I ask lots of questions, I'll know what is true.

Jesus As a Boy

*Jesus grew both in height and in wisdom, and he was loved
by God and by all who knew him.*
Luke 2:52, NLT

Jesus was God's Son, so you'd think he'd be supersmart and superstrong. But Jesus was also a person, just like you. Maybe he had freckles or hair that stuck up in funny places. Maybe he was shy or liked to read. We don't know much about Jesus' life as a child. But we do know he had to listen to his parents, learn how to get along with others, and do all the other things kids have to do. If you feel alone sometimes, remember that Jesus knows what it's like to be a kid. After all, he was young once too.

**Jesus was young like me for a while.
He knows what it's like to be a child.**

Love Your Enemies

Love your enemies! Do good to them!
Luke 6:35, TSLB

Jesus taught his followers a new way to treat people. Usually when people hurt you, you want to hurt them back. If people don't like you, you don't like them either. But Jesus tells us to love our enemies. It's never easy, but Jesus can help you. If you do good to your enemies, you could change your life and theirs—forever.

When someone is mean, I pray that I'll find
Love in my heart and strength to be kind.

Jesus' Example

Forgive, and you will be forgiven.
Luke 6:37, NIV

How do you learn to do new things? Many times it's by watching others. You can learn to ride a bike, play catch, or even skip by watching someone else do it and then trying it yourself. It's the same way with learning to forgive people when they do something wrong. We learn to forgive by watching and learning how Jesus forgave others. The more you learn about how Jesus acted, the more forgiving you'll be toward others.

Forgiving is hard when someone does wrong.
But I can watch Jesus and follow along.

Filled with Light

If you are filled with light, with no dark corners, then your whole life
will be radiant, as though a floodlight is shining on you.
Luke 11:36, NLT

It's almost impossible to stay inside on a sunny day. A clear blue sky and lots of sunshine practically beg you to come out and play. And when people see the light of Jesus' love shining through you, they'll be drawn to you, too. They'll want to know where all your happiness and joy come from. You can tell them that when Jesus lives in your heart, every day is full of sunshine!

When your heart is filled with joy and love,
You'll shine with light from God above.

Too Many to Count!

God even knows how many hairs you have on your head.
Luke 12:7, ICB

Do you know how much hair you have? Do your mum and dad know? You could try counting every single hair on your head, but you'd never figure it out. There are just too many! But God pays such close attention to you that he knows how many hairs you have. And he knows everything else about you too. Isn't it nice to have someone care so much about you?

Although I can't count all of my hairs,
They can remind me that God always cares.

A Careful Search

What woman, having ten silver coins, if she loses one coin, does not . . .
search carefully until she finds it?
Luke 15:8, NKJV

Doesn't it drive you crazy when you can't find a favourite toy? You can't stop thinking about it. You'll pull off the couch cushions, dig through your toy box, even crawl under your bed until you find your toy. God feels the same way about us, but even more strongly. We are all very important to him. When God knows even one of us is lost or in trouble or not following him, he searches for us until we're safely home with him again.

If you ever get lost, you soon will be found.
God will make sure you stay safe and sound.

A Tiny Seed

If you had faith as small as a mustard seed . . .
Luke 17:6, NLT

Jesus' followers wanted to know how they could have more faith in God. So Jesus used a mustard seed as an example. Why a mustard seed? Because it's one of the tiniest seeds around. But it's alive and growing. When it's planted in the ground, it begins to take root and then spread. Like the tiny mustard seed, a small amount of faith will take root and grow inside of you. Soon it will spread and will produce good results in your life. Thank God for the tiny seed of faith growing in you!

My faith might be small and hard to see,
But it's always alive and growing in me!

Alive Again!

[Jesus] has risen from the dead!
Luke 24:6, NLT

God the Father sent his Son, Jesus, to live with us on earth. Jesus showed us how to love others and forgive them. He taught us how to be kind to people who are different from us. But he also did something *really* amazing. Jesus was put to death for the wrong things we've done, but he didn't stay dead. God brought him back to life again. God did this to show us that Jesus is more powerful than death!

And we can live forever in heaven with him too if we trust him and ask him to forgive us.

God can do anything—yes, he can.
He even made Jesus alive again!

From the Beginning

Before anything else existed, there was Christ, with God.
He has always been alive and is himself God.
John 1:1-2, TLB

Remember at the very beginning of this book where you read about God creating the whole universe? Even way back then, at the beginning of time, Jesus was with God his Father in heaven. That means Jesus knows all about people's lives, from Adam and Eve on. He also knows how much God loves us and cares for us. And he feels the same way.

Jesus wasn't just a man who lived on the earth for a little while. He's been around since the first day of time, and just like God, he'll be with you until the last.

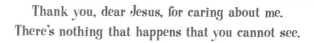

Thank you, dear Jesus, for caring about me.
There's nothing that happens that you cannot see.

You Are Valuable

For God so loved the world that he gave his only Son, so that everyone who believes in him will not perish but have eternal life.
John 3:16, NLT

When we really want something, sometimes we have to be willing to give up a lot to get it. When something is that important, we say it's "valuable." And in God's eyes, we are the most valuable of all. So what did God give up to make sure we could spend forever with him in heaven? He gave up his Son, Jesus. It must have been hard for God to send us his Son, when he knew Jesus would have to die for the wrong things we've done. But he thinks we're worth it!

God sent us his Son so we could live.
What a wonderful gift for God to give!

Drink Up!

Whoever drinks the water I give him will never thirst.
John 4:14, NIV

What's the one thing every living creature needs to live? No, not ice cream. It's water! When we don't get enough water to drink, we get very, very thirsty. That's how our bodies remind us to keep drinking. Jesus said that following him and loving him is like drinking water. Just like we need water, we also need him to live. And when we don't get enough of him, our hearts get thirsty for his love. If you follow Jesus, he promises your heart will never be thirsty again.

Come to God's fountain and you'll never thirst.
He'll fill you up. Just put Jesus first!

More Than Enough

[Jesus] gave them as much as they wanted.
John 6:11, ICB

One day a huge crowd of people came to listen to Jesus. When the people got hungry, Jesus' friends looked around for some food to give them. But all they had was a few loaves of bread and a couple of fish. Then something incredible happened. Somehow Jesus turned this small amount into enough food to feed thousands of people. And they even had leftovers! Jesus did a lot of amazing things to show people that God would always take care of them.

When Jesus gave the crowd something to eat,
A few loaves and fishes became quite a treat!

The Brightest Light

I am the light of the world.
John 8:12, NLT

What's the brightest light you can think of? Spotlights are very bright, and they can light large areas. But can you imagine a light bright enough to light up the whole world at one time? Jesus told his followers that he was the Light of the World. He shines out to all people, showing them the way to true life. God's love is so strong and bright that it lights up the whole world. And when you have God's love living inside of you, you can light up your corner of the world too!

Jesus brings light to the darkest of places.
His love is a light that will shine on our faces.

Listening for God's Voice

The sheep listen to the voice of the shepherd. . . .
They follow him because they know his voice.
John 10:3-4, ICB

Do you have a dog, a cat, or any other pet? If you do, you know that they get used to the sound of your voice. Some animals can even tell where you are in the house just by listening for your voice. When you want to find God, you just need to listen for his voice. You can hear it when you read the Bible, when you go to church, when you say your prayers, and when you enjoy the wind, rain, and birds outside. The more you listen for God's voice, the better you will become at recognising it!

The more you listen, the more you'll hear
And soon you'll know God is very near!

The Very Best Life

My purpose is to give life in all its fullness.
John 10:10, NLT

When you have a family that loves you, friends to play with, and a beautiful world to live in, you can be really thankful. But none of those things would matter if you didn't have God's love to top it all off. With God in your heart, you've got the very best life you could ask for. God loves you no matter what, he wants to give you the best of everything, and he will watch over you for the rest of your life. What more could you ask for?

God makes my life the best it can be.
I am so glad he cares for me!

Safe and Happy

[Jesus said,] "I am the good shepherd."
John 10:11, ICB

Lambs are cute, but they aren't very smart. If no one is around to take care of them, they get lost and scared, and they get into trouble. That's why lambs need a shepherd to help them stay safe and happy. Sometimes people are a little like sheep. We get confused about what we should do or shouldn't do. We get scared and we get into trouble. That's why we need Jesus. He's always there to protect us and show us the right way to go.

Jesus, my shepherd, helps me do what's right.
I know he'll protect me by day and by night.

For All Time

*Anyone who believes in me, even though he dies
like anyone else, shall live again.*
John 11:25, TLB

If you've ever had a grandpa, grandma, parent, sister, or brother who died, you know it hurts to have someone you love go away. But Jesus made us a wonderful promise. He said that when we believe in him, after we die, we will live again. We won't live on earth forever. But we *will* live in heaven with God for all time. And all those people who believed in Jesus and died before us will be there too, happy to see us again.

**Although I'm sad when loved ones go away,
I'll be happy to see them again one day.**

When You Feel Sad

Jesus wept.
John 11:35, NKJV

Jesus was God's Son, but he was also a person who felt a lot of the same feelings you feel. When his good friend Lazarus died, Jesus was very, very sad. He was so sad that he cried. Even though Jesus knew that Lazarus would be in heaven one day, he still missed his friend and felt bad. When you're sad, ask Jesus to be with you and comfort you. Remember, he knows just how you feel.

When I feel very sad, I know God will care.
He knows how I feel and he'll always be there.

Teamwork

Trust in God; trust also in me.
John 14:1, NIV

When you are part of a team, you work together with all the other team members to get things done. On a sports team, all the players work together to win the game. Your family is another kind of a team. Whether it's cleaning the house or raking leaves in the garden, the work gets done faster if everyone works together. God the Father and Jesus his Son are a team too. When you talk to God, you are talking to Jesus, too. When you ask God to be a part of your life, Jesus will be too. God the Father and his Son make the greatest team of all!

God is the Father, Jesus the Son.
Thank them for all the great things they've done.

Our Heavenly Home

There are many rooms in my Father's house....
I am going there to prepare a place for you.
John 14:2, ICB

When company comes to your house, you probably have to put all your toys away and make sure your room is clean. Now imagine Jesus getting heaven ready for all his friends. Maybe he's setting up a special spot just for you or getting a feast of all your favourite foods ready. Whatever Jesus is doing, he's making sure that heaven will be a special place—just for friends like you!

Jesus is busy in heaven today,
Preparing a home I'll live in someday.

Home, Sweet Home

After I go and prepare a place for you, I will come back.
Then I will take you to be with me so that you may be where I am.
John 14:3, ICB

Jesus' friends here on earth loved him very much. So when he told them he was leaving to go back to heaven, they were sad. But he also told them that one day they'd all be together again in heaven. That's Jesus' promise to us, too.

If you believe that Jesus is God's Son, someday you'll go to heaven too. And you'll live with Jesus. You'll get to talk with him, sit with him, play with him, and sing with him. You'll get to spend forever with the very best friend you could ever have.

In heaven, I'll see Jesus face-to-face,
And live with him in that wonderful place.

Just Follow Jesus

I am the way, and the truth, and the life.
John 14:6, NASB

If you ever wonder how to get to heaven, the answer is easy. Just follow Jesus. You don't have to be especially smart or really good or perfect. All you have to do is ask Jesus to be in charge of your life. When you do, you'll be on the path to heaven. Jesus is pointing the way. All we have to do is follow.

Getting to heaven is easy, I know.
Believing in Jesus is the right way to go.

God at Work

If you ask me for anything in my name, I will do it.
John 14:14, ICB

More than anything, Jesus wants people to love his Father.
Everything he said and did while he was on earth was to help
us see and love God. Jesus says he'll do whatever we ask, as
long as it helps people grow closer to God.
When you pray, remember to ask Jesus
for things that will help others feel
God's love. Ask him to help you
be loving and patient and
kind. Then get ready
to watch God work!

God will give what you ask for in prayer.
So ask him to help you show others his care.

For a Little While

I will not leave you as orphans; I will come to you.
John 14:18, NASB

When your mum or dad goes away on a trip, it's okay to feel a little scared. When Jesus told his friends he was going away for a while, they got scared too. But he promised them he'd be with them again. Today he makes the same promise to us. Even though we can't see Jesus walking around on the earth anymore, we know he's with us. And we'll see him in heaven one day.

Jesus, you'll never leave me alone.
I look forward to your heavenly home.

The Peace Jesus Gives

*[Jesus said,] "The peace I give isn't like the peace the world gives.
So don't be troubled or afraid."*
John 14:27, TSLB

When you feel calm and peaceful, it seems like nothing can bother you. But some- times all it takes is an annoying brother or a rude sister to take that peaceful feeling away. Just remember, though, that Jesus can fill you with the kind of peace that will never go away. The peace Jesus gives makes you feel safe, calm, and happy—all at the same time. You can feel this peace even when your brother is bugging you or your day isn't going right. It's a peace that lasts and lasts.

**The peace Jesus gives me does not disappear.
No matter what happens, it's always right here!**

Sweet Fruit

You should produce much fruit and show that you are my followers.
John 15:8, ICB

How can you tell an apple tree from a pear tree? By its fruit.
Fruit trees look pretty much the same until they have fruit on
them. But when Jesus said we should bear fruit, he didn't mean
we should grow oranges out of our ears! He meant that people
will know we are his followers by the things we do and say. Our
fruit is love and kindness and patience. When we love Jesus and
live *his* way, people will see our "fruit" and know that we are
God's children.

Peace, love, and kindness are the fruit I bear.
When people see me, they know that I care!

Love and Obey

When you obey me you are living in my love. . . . I have told you this
so that you will be filled with my joy.
John 15:10-11, TSLB

What are some ways you show people you love them? Do you give them hugs and kisses? Or share your favourite toy? Or save them a seat at the table? Those are all great ways to show love. You can show your love for Jesus, too—but in a different way. Although you can't physically give him a hug, you can do what he asks you to do. You can listen to your mum and dad, or you can comfort a hurting friend. When you obey Jesus, that's the best "hug" you can give him.

Because I love Jesus, I want to obey.
I'll do what he asks me to do every day.

September

Who Do You Love?

My command is this: Love each other as I have loved you.
John 15:12, NIV

Jesus asks us to love each other. But that doesn't just mean saying "I love you." Jesus wants us to *really* act like we love others the way he does. What does that kind of love look like? When Jesus lived on earth, he loved people who were kind and people who were mean. He loved people who looked beautiful and people who looked ordinary. He loved rich people and poor people. Jesus loves you just because you're you. He wants you to love others the same way.

**Jesus loves all people, day after day.
I'll love them too, in the very same way.**

Bursting with Joy

Ask and you will receive, and your joy will be complete.
John 16:24, NIV

What should you pray about? When you're not sure, ask God to help others see Jesus in you. That's a prayer God will always answer. God can help you show his love, care, and kindness to others, even when you don't feel loving toward them. When you treat others well, you'll be filled with a wonderful joy. You'll feel so terrific, you won't be able to hold it inside. You'll want to share it with everyone around you!

When I share God's love with each girl and boy,
God fills me up with his wonderful joy.

Bumps and Bruises

Take heart, because I have overcome the world.
John 16:33, NLT

Have you ever been really scared? Like when it started to rain and thunder outside? Or when you fell off your bike and bumped your knee on the pavement? Sometimes life will give you bumps and bruises. But Jesus can help you. He can give you courage to get through those painful times. Why? Because he's bigger and stronger and greater than anything in the world. And he's watching out for you!

Bumps and bruises are a part of life too,
But Jesus is here, watching out for you!

Warm and Wonderful

You have shown me the way of life, and you will give me
wonderful joy in your presence.
Acts 2:28, NLT

There's probably no better feeling in the world than being with someone you really love. Like when you and your dad have a great afternoon playing in the garden. Or when your mum takes a little extra time to snuggle with you before bedtime. Doesn't that make you feel all warm and wonderful inside? That's how it feels to spend time with God. And the best thing is that God will be around forever!

God, it's wonderful to be with you.
You're always with me whatever I do.

A Loving King

Salvation is found in no one else.
Acts 4:12, NIV

Back in Bible times there were lots of different kings who ruled lots of different countries. If one of those kings wanted someone to be punished, that person was punished. But Jesus is a different kind of king. He's a loving king who wants us to be happy. And he knows the best way for us to be happy is to spend forever with him. Jesus is the only king who has the power to invite us to live with him in heaven. What a wonderful king!

Jesus is our Lord, our Saviour, and King.
To him our love and obedience we'll bring.

Bold Words

Lord, . . . enable your servants to speak
your word with great boldness.
Acts 4:29, NIV

Do you know what boldness means? Boldness is saying or doing something like you really mean it when you know it's the truth. But it's hard to be bold when you're afraid of what others might say or do. What if they laugh at you or make fun of you? That's why Jesus' followers asked God to help them talk about Jesus with boldness. They wanted everyone to know about Jesus' love.

God, make me bold in all I say and do.
I won't be afraid when I talk about you!

God's Grocery Store

He has shown kindness by giving you rain from heaven and crops in their seasons; he provides you with plenty of food and fills your hearts with joy.
Acts 14:17, NIV

Do you like to go to the grocery store? It's fun to push the shopping trolley down the aisle and pick out the best bananas, isn't it? But the good things you like to eat don't just come from the grocery store. Potatoes and lettuce and corn grow in farmers' fields. Apples and pears grow on trees in an orchard. And God's the one who sends lots of rain and sunshine to help them all grow. So think of the earth as God's grocery store—full of good things!

God gives me lots of good things to eat.
The earth is full of all kinds of treats!

More Than a Friend

In [God] we live and move and are.
Acts 17:28, TLB

God does so many wonderful things for us—he's a perfect friend. But he's so much more than that! God is our creator and protector. Without him, we wouldn't have a family or a home. We wouldn't even be alive. God wants us to know that we belong to him. We are his children. He loves us more than we can even imagine!

Without God in your life, you'll be sad and lonely.
So just give your heart to him—and to him only!

Tell the World

Do not be afraid, but speak, and do not keep silent, for I am with you.
Acts 18:9-10, NKJV

One of Jesus' followers was a man named Paul. Not everyone liked what Paul said about Jesus because not everyone believed Jesus was God's Son. But God spoke to Paul in a dream and told him not to be afraid. After this, Paul continued to tell everyone he could about Jesus' love. Today it can still be scary to talk about Jesus. Some people might make fun of you. But God promises to give you the courage to tell others how much Jesus loves them. So why not start today?

God, help me be brave when I talk about you.
I know you are with me whenever I do.

Strong Kids

We must help the weak.
Acts 20:35, NIV

You might be little, but you can still do a lot of big things to help others. For instance, you can help your parents take care of your younger brothers or sisters. You can make older people smile by visiting a nursing home. You can take care of your pets and cheer up a hurting friend. What's one way you can help someone today?

I might be young, but there's lots I can do
To help other people who might feel blue.

Giving and Getting

Remember the words of the Lord Jesus:
"It is more blessed to give than to receive."
Acts 20:35, NLT

We like getting presents so much that we sometimes miss out on how much fun it is to *give* presents. When you give people gifts you picked out, you're telling them how much you love them. You're telling them that they're worth thinking about and remembering. You don't have to spend money to give someone a gift like that. A hug, a card you make yourself, or even a smile can make someone else feel special.

I like to give gifts to show that I care.
God gives me so much I just have to share.

Safe at Sea

I believe God! It will be just as he said!
Acts 27:25, TLB

Remember Paul, who was afraid to talk about Jesus? With help from God, it didn't take Paul long to get lots of courage. This verse is from a story where Paul was on a boat that was caught in a storm. The other people on the boat were afraid. They thought the waves might make the boat sink and they would die. But Paul knew God would keep them safe because God had promised. Paul learned to trust God with his life. And you can too.

I can trust God to take care of me,
Just like Paul did when he was at sea.

No Doubt

God's words will always prove true and right.
Romans 3:4, TLB

As you get older, you might start to wonder if what the Bible says is really true. You might wonder if God really loves you as much as the Bible says he does. You might wonder if he'll really watch over you forever. Paul, who wrote these words, learned that God's words are always true and right. And when the Bible says that God's words are true, you know you can believe it.

Whenever I wonder if God's really there,
I'll just remember his love and his care.

Over and Over

So now, those who are in Christ Jesus are not judged guilty.
Romans 8:1, ICB

Have you ever wanted to take a toy away from your little sister? Or steal some sweets from a shop? Doing the right thing all the time isn't easy—especially when you really want something. Sometimes you might make poor choices, even when you know what you should do. But when you make mistakes, you can ask Jesus to forgive you. And you know what? He will. Not just one time, but over and over, because he loves you so much.

Jesus forgives me when I make a mistake.
He loves me no matter what choices I make.

Imagine This!

If the Holy Spirit controls your mind, there is life and peace.
Romans 8:6, NLT

Imagine playing a game with your friends. In this game, everyone is kind to each other. People take turns, share their toys, and say only nice things to one another. No one is allowed to be mean, even for a second. That sounds like a great game, doesn't it? When we let God's Spirit into our hearts he makes us feel so good that we want to be nice. Imagine a world where everybody was like that. The world would be a very nice place.

God, thank you for filling my heart with your Spirit. This news is so good, I want others to hear it!

Healthy and Happy

We . . . wait anxiously for that day when God will give us . . .
bodies that will never be sick again and will never die.
Romans 8:23, TLB

If you've ever been to a hospital, you know that hospitals are full of sick people. Even though people are healthier and live longer now than people did many years ago, we will all still get sick sometimes. But God tells us that heaven will be a very different place. There won't be any hospitals in heaven, because there won't be any sickness! Everyone will be healthy and happy in heaven.

When we get to heaven, we'll never feel bad.
We'll never get sick and we'll never be sad.

All for the Good

*We know that in everything God works for the good
of those who love him.*
Romans 8:28, ICB

Everyone has good days and bad days. One day a
friend might say something that hurts your
feelings. Another day you might make a
new friend. Whatever kind of day
you're having, you can be sure that
Jesus isn't just sitting back and
watching. He's helping you
learn and grow through
all the things that happen
to you—the good *and*
the bad.

Though things might happen that make me feel sad,
I know Jesus helps me to grow and be glad.

God on Your Side

If God is for us, who can ever be against us?
Romans 8:31, NLT

When you have a runny nose and a bad cough, you probably have to stay in bed and rest. You might start to feel lonely, especially if you see your friends having fun without you. You might feel sorry for yourself too. But the Bible says even if you feel like everything is going against you, God is always on your side. While you are getting over your cold, remember this. You'll feel better before you know it.

When I've got a sore throat and a stuffy head,
God's still on my side while I rest in bed.

More Than a Conqueror

*In all these things we are more than conquerors
through him who loved us.*
Romans 8:37, NIV

Do you
know what it means
to "conquer" something? It
means to overcome—not just by a
little, but by a lot. Once you've conquered
something, it can never beat you again.
The Bible says that God helps us conquer
everything we go through in life. Hard
times might not go away, but they can't
beat us. They can't make us lose out on
the great things God has promised us.

With God by my side, I can conquer all.
Nothing on earth can make me fall.

Together Forever

*Nothing above us, nothing below us, or anything else in the whole world
will ever be able to separate us from the love of God
that is in Christ Jesus our Lord.*
Romans 8:39, ICB

After all the love he's shown his people over thousands of years, do you think God would let anything come between him and us? No way! Nothing you can do will keep God from loving you. Even if you say something mean about someone, God still loves you. Even if you lie about taking the last lollipop, God knows what you did, but he still loves you. Never be afraid to talk to him, even when you make poor choices. As the Bible says, nothing can separate you from his love.

Nothing I do, nothing I say
Can ever take God's love away.

God's Family

Don't copy the behavior and customs of this world, but be a new and different person with a fresh newness in all you do and think.
Romans 12:2, TLB

Do your grandparents make your favourite dessert when you visit them? Or does your family tell stories after dinner? Every family has its own special way of doing things. That's true of God's family too. When we belong to God's family, we want to be kind and loving. We try to be patient and gentle with each other. How can you show you're part of God's family today?

When you're in God's family, there's plenty to do,
Like follow God's plans and have lots of fun, too.

My Own Special Gift

God has given each of us the ability to do certain things well.
Romans 12:6, TLB

Do you ever wonder what makes you so special? God says he's given every single one of us a special gift—something we can do really well. God might have made you a very kind person who helps others feel good. Maybe he made you quiet so you could be a good listener. If you don't know what special gift God has given you, ask your mum or dad or grandparents. They'll tell you just how special you really are!

What can I do that's special and new?
Whatever it is, I'll share it with you!

God's Plan

Be glad for all God is planning for you.
Romans 12:12, TLB

When God looks at you, do you know what he sees? He sees you right now, and he sees the future, too. You don't know what you'll be like when you grow up, but God does. He's got good plans for you. If you follow him and live the way he wants you to live, God will show you his plans. He'll help you find the right path for your life, and he'll lead you in the direction he wants you to go. Whatever God has in store for you, you can bet it's going to be great!

I'm following God—he's got big plans for me.
I can't wait to discover just what they will be!

Be on the Lookout

Share with God's people who need help.
Romans 12:13, ICB

If you heard someone crying for help, you'd probably run to see what was wrong. But sometimes people who need help cry out in ways we can't hear. A person who's sad might just sit quietly by herself. A person who's hungry might wait for someone to offer him food. If we pay attention to others, we can find ways to help. We can talk to the sad person who's sitting alone. We can share our food with someone who doesn't have any. If you want to help others, just keep your eyes open. You'll be surprised by what you see!

If I keep my eyes open, I know I'll see
Ways to help others like Jesus helps me.

More Than a Word

Love does no wrong to anyone.
Romans 13:10, TLB

Lots of people talk about love. But what does love mean? Love is more than just feeling good or being nice. Love means really thinking about what others need. It means being kind, even when others aren't kind to you. Love is doing what's right, even when it's hard. Jesus showed us a very special kind of love when he came to earth to live with us. He was always kind and patient. He always cared about the people he met, no matter who they were or what they were like. How can you show Jesus' kind of love?

Jesus showed love to everyone he met.
He's an example I'll never forget.

You've Got Power

Every spiritual gift and power for doing his will are yours.
1 Corinthians 1:7, TLB

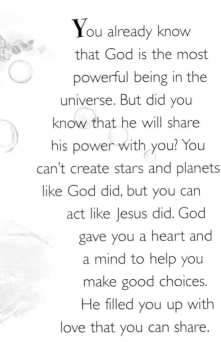

You already know that God is the most powerful being in the universe. But did you know that he will share his power with you? You can't create stars and planets like God did, but you can act like Jesus did. God gave you a heart and a mind to help you make good choices. He filled you up with love that you can share. And he gave you Jesus, so that you could follow his words and actions. Ask God to give you the power to live for him. Then just watch what happens!

I know that God will give me the power
To love and share with others each hour.

Surprise Party!

[Nobody] has ever seen, heard, or even imagined what wonderful things God has ready for those who love the Lord.
I Corinthians 2:9, TLB

When people plan a surprise birthday party, they figure out what the birthday person will want to eat, which friends they should invite, and what decorations would be fun. They make all sorts of plans to lovingly surprise the birthday person. Well, God has a great big surprise party planned for us in heaven. We don't know what we'll look like, what we'll wear, or what we'll eat. But it will be better than anything we can imagine. Why? Because God can't wait to show us how much he loves us!

When I get to heaven, a party I'll find.
What fun to see what God has in mind!

Celebrate Today!

*[God] has given you all of the present and
all of the future. All are yours.*
I Corinthians 3:22, TLB

If you think too much about the future, you might not pay
attention to the good things God gives us each day. Even when
a day seems ordinary, it's a special gift from God. Listening to
water trickle from a tap, following a ladybird as it flits
across the yard, or playing in the sand at the beach
might not seem all that exciting. But that water,
that ladybird, and that sand are all gifts
from God. And you can
enjoy them fully!

Each day is a gift from God to me.
There's so much to do and so much to see.

The Way Out

When you are tempted, he will show you a way out
so that you will not give in to it.
1 Corinthians 10:13, NLT

When you feel like doing something you know you shouldn't,
God promises to help you find a way out of trouble. If a friend
wants you to be mean to another friend, God will help you say
no. If your brother asks you to tell a lie, God will help you be
honest. When you feel tempted, go to God.
He'll help you find the way out. He'll
help you do the right thing.

When I'm headed for trouble and losing my way,
God helps me out—I just have to pray.

Gifts from God

*God gives us many kinds of special abilities,
but it is the same Holy Spirit who is the source of them all.*
1 Corinthians 12:4, TLB

Have you ever known people who brag about all the great things they can do? When you hear people brag, just remember that it's God who gave them the ability to do those great things. And God gave you special abilities too. Some people can draw really well and others can sing beautifully. Some kids are great at sports and other kids can tell wonderful stories. It doesn't matter what you're good at. All the gifts we have are from God. And that's what matters most.

God gave us all something special to do.
I have his gifts, and others do, too.

October

Wait Your Turn

Love is patient.
1 Corinthians 13:4, NIV

Is it ever hard to wait your turn? Sometimes you have to stand in a line to get a hot dog at a football game when you're *really* hungry. Or you have to wait for your brother to finish playing with his skateboard so you can have a turn. Waiting isn't easy. You can get really frustrated. But the Bible says that being patient and waiting your turn is another way to show love to others. So the next time you have to wait, sing a song, say a prayer, or just remember this verse. And then your turn will come faster than you think!

Sometimes it's hard to wait for my turn,
But patience is something God wants me to learn.

Acts of Kindness

Love is kind.
1 Corinthians 13:4, NIV

Has someone ever done something nice for you? Maybe your brother shared his favourite truck. Or a friend drew a picture for you when you were sick. Doing something nice is one way to show others how special they are. So when you love people and you want them to know it, do something kind for them. Set the table for your mum. Tie your little sister's shoes. Hug your dad. When you show others you love them, you'll feel good, too.

When I am kind, I'm showing my love,
The love that's a gift from God up above.

The Best Kind of Friend

Love does not demand its own way.
It is not irritable or touchy. It does not hold grudges.
1 Corinthians 13:5, TLB

What kind of friend do you like to spend time with? That's easy—the kind of friend who shares his sweets with you and who lets you ride his bike. It's hard to be friends with a person who always wants everything to be her way. A good friend thinks of others first. So if your friend feels like playing with dolls when you want to play dressing-up, take turns. If you want to sit by the teacher during story time but someone else gets there first, try not to pout. Be the kind of friend who takes turns and shares. Then you'll always have lots of friends.

Instead of pushing so things go my way,
I'll think first of others when I want to play.

A Big Boost

Love never gives up.
I Corinthians 13:7, NLT

What does your mum or dad say when you're learning to do
something new? Maybe, "Great try!" Or, "You can do it!" Their
words might not help you figure out how to tie your shoes
faster or hit a ball better, but they do help you feel good.
When you love people, you can show it by sticking with them
and encouraging them. If your best friend is trying to read or
your little sister is learning to button her coat, let them know
you believe they can do it. Your loving words will
give them a big boost.

When you believe others really can do it,
You'll do your best to help them get through it!

Love First

Let love be your greatest aim.
I Corinthians 14:1, TLB

Have you got big plans for tomorrow? Like playing catch with a friend? Or running through the crunchy autumn leaves? Or watching your favourite video? Whatever you do tomorrow, do it with love. You see, of all the things you do each day, the most important of all is to love others.

So when you're playing catch, be kind to your friend. When you run in the leaves, ask your brother to join you. When you turn on that video, snuggle up next to your mum. Then everyone will have a great day!

Whatever you do, you can do it with love.
It's God's biggest rule from heaven above.

A New Life

In Christ all shall be made alive.
I Corinthians 15:22, NKJV

When someone you love dies, you feel sad because you'll miss that person a lot. But when we believe in Jesus, death isn't the end for us. Someday we'll see each other again in heaven. That means even though you feel sad now, you don't have to say good-bye forever. You'll get to join the person you miss in heaven someday—where there is no sadness or pain or tears. And then you can say hello again. Won't that be wonderful?

When I get to heaven God says that I'll see
All those who love him and always loved me.

An Amazing Place!

[Our bodies] are weak now, but when they are raised,
they will be full of power.
1 Corinthians 15:43, NLT

Do you know anyone who uses a wheelchair or has a hard time seeing or hearing? Our bodies don't always do the things we want them to do, at least not here on earth. But if we love God, someday we'll live in heaven with him, and we'll have bodies that work perfectly. Imagine never getting sick or hurt, never breaking a bone or stubbing a toe. Even people who can't walk now will run in heaven. It's going to be an amazing place!

When we get to heaven, we'll all feel so good.
Our bodies will work just the way that they should.

Jesus Is the Answer

For no matter how many promises God has made,
they are "Yes" in Christ.
2 Corinthians 1:20, NIV

God made lots of
promises in the Old
Testament. God
promised Noah,
who built the
ark, that he would
always forgive people
when they asked him
to and never punish
them with
another flood.
God promised King David
that someone from his family would
rule Israel forever. And you know what? That promise
came true when Jesus, God's Son, came to earth. He's the ruler
God promised. And most of all, Jesus came to bring us God's
forgiveness. Jesus is the ultimate sign of God's love.

Promises for you and promises for me.
God's promises are true in Jesus, you see!

Marked for God

*He has put his brand upon us—his mark of ownership—
and given us his Holy Spirit in our hearts
as guarantee that we belong to him.*
2 Corinthians 1:22, TLB

Have you ever written your name on something that belongs to you—just to make sure no one else takes it? That's what God does for us when we tell him we love him. Because he loves us so much, he calls us his children. And he sends his Spirit to live inside each of us. By loving those around us, we can let everyone know we belong to God.

I am God's child and to him I belong.
I'll show his great love the whole day long.

Not-So-Good Days

The troubles will soon be over, but the joys to come will last forever.
2 Corinthians 4:18, TLB

Most days you feel happy when you wake up. But every once in a while, a day just seems to start out badly. Maybe you can't find your favourite shirt, or you get eggs for breakfast when you really wanted pancakes. Or maybe your sister gets mad at you for playing with her toys, and no one has time to read you a story. On days like this, remember God promises that in heaven every day will be perfect. And you won't have to worry about things like lost shirts or not-so-good breakfasts ever again.

On earth there are days both good and bad,
But nothing in heaven will make me sad.

New Clothes

We long for the day when we will put on our
heavenly bodies like new clothing.
2 Corinthians 5:2, NLT

You are growing bigger and taller all the time. Before you know it, you've outgrown all your clothes. Suddenly it's time for your mum to take you shopping and buy you some brand-new clothes. New clothes are great—they can make *you* feel brand-new too! The Bible says our body is a little like clothing. When our time on earth is over, our body will be like old clothes that we've outgrown. And when we get to heaven, we will put on new clothes—our brand-new heavenly bodies!

Heaven's so perfect, I hardly can wait.
I'll have a new body, and life will be great!

The Joy of Giving

God loves the person who gives cheerfully.
2 Corinthians 9:7, NLT

Don't you just *love* to get a present? You smile as you look at the brightly coloured paper and the bow. You wonder what's inside. And then you get to open it. What fun! But did you know that *giving* presents can be as much fun as *getting* them? When you give someone a special gift, give it with joy. And your gift doesn't even have to be wrapped. It can even be something as simple as a hug or a smile.

When you give gifts with a heart full of joy,
You'll show God's love to each girl and each boy.

Enough to Share

God will generously provide all you need. Then you will always have
everything you need and plenty left over to share with others.
2 Corinthians 9:8, NLT

Do you have more than one toy? When you have a snack, do you get more than one biscuit or a great big apple? God will always make sure we have the things we need, like a warm place to sleep and clothes to wear. So when you're asked to share what you have with someone else, don't worry that there won't be enough left for you. God promises you'll always have what you need.

I'll always have plenty of good things to share,
Whether toys to play with or clothes to wear!

OCTOBER 14

God's Power in You

[Jesus] said, . . ."My power shows up best in weak people."
2 Corinthians 12:9, TLB

Have you ever seen a kid who acted tough or who was always swaggering around, trying to impress others? You might think you have to be tough, or strong, or perfect to impress people. But God says it's okay to be weak. God says his power shows up best in people who need him most. So we never have to worry about being something we're not. We can be ourselves and trust God to show his power in us!

I need God, I'm not scared to say,
His power in me shows up best this way!

A Big, Happy Family

You are all children of God through faith in Christ Jesus.
Galatians 3:26, ICB

If you have a brother or a sister, you know that it's a lot of fun to have someone in your family you can play with, laugh with, and share secrets with. But did you know that every person who loves God is your brother or sister too? That means you've got brothers and sisters in China, Africa, India, and South America! God loves all his children and wants us to love each other. Isn't it great to have family all over the world?

My brothers and sisters aren't just in my home.
I can find family wherever I roam.

Showing Love

The only thing that counts is faith expressing itself through love.
Galatians 5:6, NIV

People show their love for God in lots of different ways. Some people like to be by themselves and think quietly about God. Other people like to gather with friends and family to sing songs to him. Some people like to read special prayers in prayer books. Other people like to tell God whatever they're thinking. There's no right or wrong way to show God you love him. All that matters is that you do it!

We all love God in our own special way,
And we can show him our love every day.

Growing Good Fruit

[The Holy Spirit] will produce this kind of fruit in us: love, joy, peace, patience, kindness, goodness, faithfulness, gentleness, and self-control.
Galatians 5:22-23, NLT

When God's Spirit lives in our hearts, God's love shows in our lives. Just like the fruit growing on a tree tells you what kind of tree it is, the good "fruit" that shows in your life tells people what kind of person you are. When you're loving, kind, patient, and all the other things this verse talks about, you show people that you are part of God's family. That's the kind of good fruit that attracts others to God.

God, help me grow "fruit" so others can see
How much of your Spirit is living in me.

A Friend in Need

Share each other's troubles and problems.
Galatians 6:2, TLB

If you're playing a game and someone gets hurt, you stop playing and try to help that person, don't you? Well, sometimes people get hurt on the inside. Those inside hurts show up in your friend's tears or sad face. When friends are hurt, on the outside or the inside, you can show your love by helping them. If a friend is sad, give her a hug. If a friend is being picked on, stay by his side. Whatever you do to help your friends, you'll be sharing their problems—just like this verse says!

When someone needs help, I can show them I care
By hugging or listening or just being there.

Well Done!

Be sure to do what you should, for then you will enjoy the personal satisfaction of having done your work well, and you won't need to compare yourself to anyone else.
Galatians 6:4, NLT

When you're young, it seems like everyone can do things better than you can. Your older friends can ride bikes, but you still need stabilisers. Your older brother can write his name, but you still need help. Even though you can't do everything older kids can do, try to do your very best at the things you *can* do. And before you know it, you'll be big enough to do all those other things too!

I can't do everything, that much is true,
But I'll do my best at the things I can do.

Sow and Grow

You will always reap what you sow!
Galatians 6:7, NLT

If you plant daisy seeds in your garden, what do you think will grow? Daisies, of course! The Bible tells us that whatever we plant in our heart is what will grow in our life. So if you fill your heart with mean thoughts or bad feelings, it will be hard for you to be the kind, loving person God wants you to be. But if you let God fill your heart with his love and care, you'll be able to show love and care to others. Let God plant good things in your heart and watch what grows!

My heart is full of God's great love and care,
So I can share love with my friends everywhere.

Surprise, Surprise!

We must not become tired of doing good.
Galatians 6:9, ICB

Have you ever surprised your mum or dad by setting the dinner table—even before being asked? Or surprised your big brother by taking out the rubbish so he could sleep later? Doing good for others is a lot of fun—especially when you go beyond what's expected of you. But sometimes it's hard to do good when you feel tired or grumpy yourself. But those are exactly the times you *need* to do good for others, because it will make you feel better too!

Do something nice just out of the blue,
Especially if it's not expected of you!

Everything You Need

*[God] has blessed us with every blessing in heaven
because we belong to Christ.*
Ephesians 1:3, TLB

Who owns everything that's in your house? Your mum or dad? Although they probably bought most of the things you have, they still let you eat the food they buy and live in the house they paid for. They share the things they own because you are their child and they love you. Well, God shares everything he has with you—even great things like the beautiful world he created—just because you are his child! He gives you everything you need because you are part of his heavenly family.

God shares all the wonders of heaven with me.
He gives great things to his whole family.

What's Best for You

How well he understands us and knows what is best for us at all times.
Ephesians 1:8, TLB

Your mum and dad know you pretty well.
They know what makes you happy,
and they know what makes you sad. But God
knows you even better. He knows everything
that's going on in your heart. He even knows
things about you that you don't know, like
what you need to feel good and be happy.
That's why it's so important to
trust God. He'll always take
care of you, your whole
life long. Even when
you don't know
what you want
or need, God
does. And he'll
make sure you always
have what's best for you.

God knows what I'm feeling deep down in my heart.
He knew what was best for me right from the start!

The Power of Love

May you experience the love of Christ, though it is so great you will never fully understand it. Then you will be filled with the fullness of life and power that comes from God.
Ephesians 3:19, NLT

Did you know that the love of Jesus is so powerful, it actually gives us life? It's true that lots of people live without Jesus. But look at all they're missing! They don't know that Jesus loves them no matter what, knows everything about them, and forgives them even when they do something wrong. But with Jesus in your heart, your life is full of wonderful things, like peace and joy and happiness.

My heart's so full of Jesus' love and his power,
My life just gets better and better each hour!

More Than We Can Imagine!

[God] is able to do immeasurably more than all we ask or imagine, according to his power that is at work within us.
Ephesians 3:20, NIV

Can you think of anything that God can't do? Can he move a mountain? Can he calm a storm? Can he make the ocean split in two? The Bible says God can do all these things and more. It's hard for us to understand just how powerful God is. But we can trust that God will always use his power to help us. He can do things we can't even imagine. There's nothing he can't do!

If God can move mountains and do even more,
I just can't imagine what else is in store!

Making a Friend

Always be humble and gentle. Be patient and accept each other with love.
Ephesians 4:2, ICB

If you're like most kids, you pick friends who are fun to be with, who like the same things you like, and who are nice to you. As great as it is to *have* good friends, it's even better to *be* a good friend. When you are kind and gentle to others, they'll love being your friends. And when you like your friends just the way they are, they'll stay your friends for a long time.

Having a friend seems as good as it gets.
But being a friend is still better yet.

Forgiving One Another

Be kind to each other, tenderhearted, forgiving one another,
just as God through Christ has forgiven you.
Ephesians 4:32, NLT

Have you ever been so mad at someone you just wanted to scream? When your sister ruins the picture you've been working on all afternoon or your little brother breaks your favourite toy, it's easy to get really, really angry. But God wants us to forgive our brothers and sisters and friends and parents—even when they make us mad. God forgives us every time we make a mistake. We just have to ask him. And he wants us to do the same for others. The next time you're angry at someone, ask God to help you forgive that person.

God, help me forgive my family and friends
With kindness and love that never will end.

Favourite Gifts

Always give thanks to God the Father for everything.
Ephesians 5:20, ICB

What are some of your favourite things? Do you like snowflakes? How about feathers or piles of leaves? All the things you love are gifts from God. From fluffy clouds in the sky to rich black dirt in the ground, God gives you many wonderful things to enjoy. The next time you're enjoying one of your favourite things, be sure to say, "Thanks, God!"

Thank you for snowballs and blue skies and mittens,
Friendship and feathers and small, fluffy kittens!

God Notices

Remember that the Lord will reward each one of us for the good we do.
Ephesians 6:8, NLT

Sometimes the nice things we do don't even get noticed. You might make your bed, but your mum or dad doesn't see it. You might draw a butterfly and give it to a friend, but he doesn't say thank you. But even when others don't notice the good things you do, God does. And he'll have a wonderful reward waiting for you in heaven.

When I do good things, I know that God sees.
My reward is in heaven, just waiting for me.

Friends Are Special

I thank God every time I remember you.
Philippians 1:3, ICB

Do you have a special friend who always makes you feel good? Maybe it's your grandma or your neighbour or a friend from school. When you spend time with your friend, or even when you're just thinking about how much you love that person, say a little thank-you prayer to God. And then tell that person how much you appreciate him or her too! A special friend is one of the very best gifts God can give you.

I love my friends, and I'll tell them I do.
I'll also tell God by saying, "Thank you!"

God's Not Finished Yet

*God, who began the good work within you, will continue his work until
it is finally finished on that day when Christ Jesus comes back again.*
Philippians 1:6, NLT

It takes time to make something really special. When you paint
a beautiful picture or build a fort, you have to put a lot of time
into it to get it just right. Well, to God you're a
beautiful creation. He's put a
lot of time into making
you just right too, and
he's not done yet.
Each day God helps
you learn something
new. And he helps
you grow closer
to him.

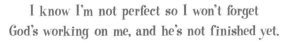

I know I'm not perfect so I won't forget
God's working on me, and he's not finished yet.

November

The Power to Please

*For God is working in you, giving you the desire to obey him
and the power to do what pleases him.*
Philippians 2:13, NLT

When you think about obeying God, you might feel like there are just too many rules. Maybe you think you can't possibly be as good as God wants you to be. But God doesn't expect you to be good and obedient all by yourself. First God puts deep in your heart a strong desire to do what pleases him. And then he gives you all the power you need to love and obey him. With his great help, you can't lose!

God is working deep within me,
Giving me all the power I need!

Thanks, God!

Tell God your needs, and don't forget to thank him for his answers.
Philippians 4:6, TLB

God loves it when you tell him what you need. But he also loves it when you thank him for all the things he does for you. When you talk to God, go ahead and tell him about your day. Tell him what annoyed you and what went great. Tell him what you'd like him to help you with. But also spend some time telling him how much you love all the good things he gives you, like sunshine and parents and friends. Don't forget to thank him!

God loves to hear all the things that you say,
But remember to thank him each time that you pray.

Recipe for a Happy Heart

Fix your thoughts on what is true and good and right.
Philippians 4:8, TLB

If you mix pickle juice, raisins, dirt, olives, old bread, and sour cream together, what will you get? A big mess! And certainly not chocolate biscuits! The things you mix together make a big difference. The same is true for what you put in your mind and heart. So if you want your heart and mind to be filled with goodness, you have to put good things into them. Instead of thinking about scary things or mean things or sad things, think about all the wonderful things God has given you and all the love he has for you. That's a recipe for a happy heart!

Thinking thoughts both good and true
Makes happy hearts for me and you!

Learn and Go

Keep putting into practice all you learned.
Philippians 4:9, NLT

All the things you learn from the Bible are wonderful, but they really only matter if you practice doing what you've learned. So when God says to love your neighbour, go out and help a friend. When God says to obey your parents, do your chores with a smile. When God says to be kind to others, share your toys with your brothers and sisters. All the valuable things God teaches us are meant to be put into action. So get going!

The Bible is full of great ways to show
God's love to all of the people we know.

Strong in God

I can do all things through Christ because he gives me strength.
Philippians 4:13, ICB

God helped
Moses and Abraham and David and
Jonah and many others in the Bible. The Old Testament is full of
their exciting stories. No matter what kind of trouble they were
in, God was on their side. God gave them the strength they
needed to fight wars and save entire nations. And he'll give you
all the strength you need too. You can trust God. He's been
helping his people forever.

Moses trusted God, and I can, too.
Just like Moses, I know God is true!

More Than You Need

[God] will supply all your needs from his glorious riches.
Philippians 4:19, NLT

When the Bible says God has riches, it doesn't mean that he has piles of money. It means that he's rich with love and power—and he uses his love and power to give each of us just what we need. He might not give you a pony or a swimming pool, but he'll surround you with people who care about you. He'll give you the promise of his love and forgiveness forever and ever. When God takes care of your needs, you'll feel rich too!

God's rich in love and rich in power—
He gives me all I need each hour.

Jesus Understands

He is the image of the invisible God, the firstborn over all creation.
For by him all things were created. . . . In him all things hold together.
Colossians 1:15-17, NIV

When Jesus lived on the earth, he wasn't just a really nice man who loved people. He was, and still is, God's Son. Jesus was God in a human body, a person who knew what it's like to be a child, a teenager, and a grown-up. Because of Jesus, we know that God understands the world and the people in it.

Jesus lived as a man, he was human like me.
He knows how life on earth can be!

No More Grudges

Be gentle and ready to forgive; never hold grudges.
Colossians 3:13, TLB

Do you know what a grudge is? It's hanging on to the bad feelings you have about the way someone treated you. If a friend takes your toy and two weeks later you're still mad at her, that's a grudge. God wants you to let go of your grudges and forgive those who hurt you. If you do, God will be happy and you will be, too. You'll feel so much better when you get rid of your grudge!

I'll never hold grudges, it just won't do,
When it's so much nicer forgiving you!

Why Obey?

Children, obey your parents in all things.
Colossians 3:20, ICB

God wants you to obey your parents, even when you don't want to. Sometimes they ask you to get dressed, but you'd rather play. Or they tell you to eat your dinner, but you only want dessert. God gave you parents so that you'd grow up healthy and happy. When your parents ask you to do something—or tell you not to do something—God wants you to obey them. They're taking care of you, just like God wants them to.

My parents take care of me, just like they should.
I want to obey them and try to be good.

With All Your Heart

Whatever you do, work at it with all your heart.
Colossians 3:23, NIV

When you need to clean up your room, have you ever shoved your stuff under the bed instead of putting it away? Even though having a clean room is not the most important thing in the world, God wants you to put your best effort into everything you do. Even if you don't do things perfectly, you'll know in your heart that you've done the best you can. And that's all God, and your parents, ask for.

Whatever I do, I will give it my best,
And then I'll trust God to take care of the rest.

A Good Example

Honor those who . . . work hard among you and warn you against all
that is wrong. Think highly of them and give them your wholehearted love.
1 Thessalonians 5:12-13, NLT

Does your grandma love to talk to Jesus every day? Is your older sister always kind to others? People who live for God and show his love to others help all of us remember to do the same. If you're willing to learn from them and follow their example, they'll help you grow closer to God. And who knows? Someone might follow your example too!

God, thanks for those who teach me about you.
They help me to love you in all that I do.

Be Good to Each Other

Be sure that no one pays back wrong for wrong.
But always try to do what is good for each other.
I Thessalonians 5:15, ICB

When someone hurts your feelings, it's natural to want to hurt them back. But that just leaves two people with hurt feelings. Instead of hurting someone who's hurt you, try doing something nice for that person instead, like sharing a page of your colouring book or asking her to play catch with you. You'll be surprised at how good it feels to "do good"!

When someone I know tries to hurt me or fight,
Instead I'll do good, 'cause I know that's what's right.

A "Thanks" Hunt

No matter what happens, always be thankful,
for this is God's will for you who belong to Christ Jesus.
I Thessalonians 5:18, TLB

If you lost your favourite cuddly toy, it would be pretty hard to be thankful, wouldn't it? But the Bible tells us to be thankful, no matter what. Even when something hard happens, God can help us find something to be grateful for. Like that cuddly toy. Even if it's gone, you could be thankful you had it for a little while. And you can always be thankful for God's comfort while you're sad. Why not go on a "thanks" hunt each day? What can you be grateful for today?

Every morning, when I see a new day,
I can be thankful at work and at play!

A Heavenly Kid

God, who called you to become his child,
will do all this for you, just as he promised.
I Thessalonians 5:24, TLB

God is so powerful, he can have anything he wants. But do you know what he wants most of all? You! You're not just something he made one day when he was bored. You are his special child, someone he loves so much that he can't wait for you to live with him forever. That's why he will always keep his promise to watch over you, guide you, protect you, love you, and forgive you. That's what a heavenly Father does for his kids.

God is my Father, my guide, and my friend.
He says he'll watch over me until the end.

As Good As Can Be

God will make you the kind of children he wants to have—
will make you as good as you wish you could be!
2 Thessalonians 1:11, TLB

What puts you in a really good mood? Eating pizza with your dad? Or playing games with your sister? Now think about how you feel when you're in a really bad mood. Let's say it's time to go to bed, but you don't feel tired. So you stamp your feet and shout and cry. But you still have to go to bed. It's much nicer to be in a good mood, isn't it? You can be, too, because God promises to help you be just as good as you want to be!

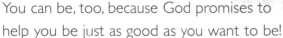

When I do what's right, my mood is so bright.
I'm as good as can be, and full of God's light!

Whatever the Weather

The Lord is faithful, and he will strengthen and protect you.
2 Thessalonians 3:3, NIV

Sometimes the weather is just perfect, isn't it? Clear blue skies, lots of bright sunshine, crisp fall air. And sometimes the weather is just the opposite, with loud crashes of thunder, bright bolts of lightning, heavy rain, and snow. In some places there are even tornadoes, hurricanes, or earthquakes. But no matter how scary the weather might seem, always remember that God is stronger than anything. He promises to protect you, no matter what!

Whether sunshine and blue skies or rain in the air,
I'm glad God's protection is everywhere!

A Heart Full of Love

The goal of this command is love, which comes from a pure heart
and a good conscience and a sincere faith.
I Timothy 1:5, NIV

Have you ever pretended to be sick to get a little extra attention? Or faked crying to get your way? You can fake a lot of things, but you can't fake love. Love is something that bubbles up from what's inside you. If your heart is full of bad feelings or angry thoughts, it's hard for love to come out. But when your heart is full of God, love can't help but pour out of you. So go ahead—let love spill out of your full heart!

My heart's full of love, and I want to share it.
Keep it inside? Oh, I just couldn't bear it!

God Uses You!

Don't let anyone look down on you because you are young.
I Timothy 4:12, NIV

Even when you're little, God can do big things through you. He can use the joy you feel every day to help older people feel joyful, too. He can use your excitement about the world to remind adults how wonderful his creation is. And he can use your tender heart to show grown-ups what real love is like. God has lots of plans for you, and guess what? They start right now!

I might be young, but there's lots I can do.
God can use me in his big kingdom, too.

Long-Distance Love

I always remember you in my prayers, day and night.
And I thank God for you in these prayers.
2 Timothy 1:3, ICB

When someone you love lives far away, it's not always easy to show them how much you care about them. But one of the wonderful things about being part of God's big family is that we can ask God to give extra love to the people we love. When you say your prayers tonight, ask God to give a little extra love to your grandparents or your cousins or your aunt and uncle who live far away. No matter how far away they are, God's arms of love are long enough to reach them.

The people I love might live far away,
But I can still pray for them every day.

Full of Courage

For God has not given us a spirit of fear and timidity,
but of power, love, and self-discipline.
2 Timothy 1:7, NLT

Do you get nervous when you try something new? Maybe you really want to learn to swim, but that deep water is still a little scary. Or maybe you worry when your parents leave you with a baby-sitter for a few hours. When you feel scared, ask God to fill you with courage. When you've got his power and confidence in you, there's nothing to be afraid of!

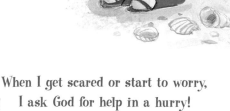

When I get scared or start to worry,
I ask God for help in a hurry!

Always Faithful

Even when we are too weak to have any faith left, he remains faithful to us and will help us . . . and he will always carry out his promises to us.
2 Timothy 2:13, TLB

Some days you feel full of energy and full of faith. But other days you might feel weak and tired with no faith left! Either way, God is still with you. There's nothing you can do that will make God stop loving you and caring for you. If you love God, you will always be part of God's family. He'll never let you go.

God is faithful, even when I am not.
I'm part of his family—I'm loved a lot!

A Ready Helper

Since he himself has gone through suffering and temptation,
he is able to help us when we are being tempted.
Hebrews 2:18, NLT

When Jesus lived on earth, he experienced the same kinds of feelings you do. He got angry and he felt sad. People tried to get him to do things he knew he shouldn't. So Jesus knows what it feels like to be hurt or to be tempted. When you feel bad, or when you're thinking about doing something you know is wrong, talk to Jesus about it. He knows how you feel, and he's ready to help. Just ask him!

When I'm tempted to do what I know is not right,
I'll call on Jesus, whether it's day or night.

Words of Life

The word of God is full of living power.
Hebrews 4:12, NLT

Have you ever noticed how your favourite stories come to life when you read them? When you're out walking in the woods, you can almost picture the creatures from your story books romping through the forest, or swinging from the trees. The stories in the Bible come to life too. Every time you live the way the Bible tells you to, you're helping people see that God's Word is more than just letters on a page. It's full of real power.

The Bible is really God's powerful Word,
Each lively story just waits to be heard!

The King of All

*Let us therefore draw near with confidence to the throne of grace,
that we may receive mercy and may find grace to help in time of need.*
Hebrews 4:16, NASB

Imagine living in a country that has a king and a queen. Now imagine you have a question or a problem. Would you just walk up to the powerful king and queen and say, "Hi, I need your help"? No way! But God is the greatest King of all. And he tells us we can come to him any time, with any problem. You don't have to be nervous about approaching God's throne!

I am so glad I can talk to my King.
I know I can ask him about anything!

Full of Faith

Let us draw near to God with a sincere heart in full assurance of faith.
Hebrews 10:22, NIV

The whole Bible is full of stories about God's love for his people. So when you want to talk to God, you don't need to wonder if he's mad at you for mistakes you've made. And you don't ever have to wonder if he's really listening to you. Why? Because God always loves you! And he's spent thousands of years proving how much he cares for his people. That's why you can be sure he cares for you, too!

I can be confident God cares for me.
He's loved his people throughout history!

Join Together

*Let us consider how we may spur one another
on toward love and good deeds.*
Hebrews 10:24, NIV

Because we're part of God's family, we're never
on our own. We can do all kinds of things
to help each other love God and show
his love to others. If you see a
lonely little girl on the playground,
grab a few friends and go talk
to her together. If you decide
to help your parents rake
leaves, ask your brothers
and sisters to join in.
When we work together,
we can multiply the love
we show others—
and the good
deeds, too.

Why not join in with your sisters and brothers
To show God's love together to others?

Faith Is . . .

What is faith? It is the confident assurance that something we want is going to happen. It is the certainty that what we hope for is waiting for us, even though we cannot see it up ahead.
Hebrews 11:1, TLB

*F*aith is a word that even grown-ups have a hard time understanding. But this Bible verse makes it pretty clear. Faith is believing something is true. You have faith that the sun will come up in the morning, or that you'll celebrate your birthday again this year. Since we can't see God's face or touch his hands, we have to have faith that he is real. And just like the sun, God is with us every day. You can believe it because the Bible says it's true!

God gives me the faith to know he is real.
Though I can't see him, it's his love I feel.

Just like Jesus

Keep your eyes on Jesus, our leader and instructor.
Hebrews 12:2, TLB

When you want to know how to treat others with love and how to follow God, imagine what Jesus would do. Jesus was kind to everyone. He talked to God every day. He always did the right thing, even when he was tempted to do wrong. When you aren't sure what to do, keep your eyes on Jesus. Then you can love others with the same kind of love Jesus has.

When I'm not sure what to do or to say,
I'll just watch Jesus—he'll show me the way.

A Friend for Life

I will never leave you nor forsake you.
Hebrews 13:5, NKJV

Have you ever been playing with a group of kids when suddenly they all run off and leave you alone? That's a lonely feeling. But it's a feeling you'll never have with God. No matter how tough things get in your life, or how bad you feel, God will never, ever leave you. Even if you forget to talk with him for a long time, he won't forget about you. He'll be with you every day, from now until the end of time.

God will not leave me—he'll always be near.
Each time I talk, I know that he'll hear.

A Real Helper

The Lord is my helper, so I will not be afraid.
Hebrews 13:6, NLT

Wouldn't it be cool to have an imaginary friend who could make sure nothing bad ever happened to you? Your imaginary friend could stand up to anyone who tried to hurt you, help you find things when they get lost, or even give you a hug when you're feeling bad. But Jesus is even better than an imaginary friend. He loves you and can fill you with the courage you need to handle anything that happens in your life.

Now that's a *real* friend, and a real helper, too!

With Jesus beside me, there's nothing to fear.
He's always with me, and he's very near!

December

Jesus Never Changes

Jesus Christ is the same yesterday and today and forever.
Hebrews 13:8, NIV

The Bible tells us how Jesus, who lived on the earth, loved little children. He liked to spend time with people, even if they had problems and even if they had made big mistakes. Jesus lives in heaven now, but he hasn't changed a bit. He still loves kids like you, he still wants to hear all about you, and he still wants to forgive you when you do something you shouldn't. Jesus' love for you will never change— not today, not tomorrow, not ever!

Jesus will stay the same, all of my days.
He never will change his kind, loving ways.

The Wise Choice

If any of you lacks wisdom, let him ask of God . . .
and it will be given to him.
James 1:5, NKJV

Even at your age, you have choices to make every day. Like whether or not to eat the orange in your lunch, or whether or not to turn in the lost mitten you found on the playground. As you get older, the choices will become harder, like what kind of kids you should play with. And when you become an adult, you'll be making choices about where to live or what kind of job to take. Many times you won't be sure what to do. But if you start asking God for wisdom now, it'll be easier to make good choices later. After all, God has promised to give you wisdom your whole life through.

When I have a tough choice that I have to make,
God helps me to know which path I should take!

The Best Gifts

Every good and perfect gift is from above.
James 1:17, NIV

Did you let the sun shine on your cheeks today? Did you catch a snowflake on your tongue? Did you get a hug from your dad? Every wonderful thing you did today is a gift from God. The snowflakes that melt on your tongue, the sunshine that warms your face, and the great feeling you get when someone hugs you all come from God. Who could ask for better gifts?

All of the wonderful things that I love
Are presents from God, his gifts from above.

Take It Slow

Be quick to listen, slow to speak, and slow to get angry.
James 1:19-20, NLT

When you get mad, what do you do? Do you kick or yell or cry or pout? Those things might make you feel a little better for a minute, but they don't accomplish much. If you really want to take care of a problem, it's a lot better to talk about it. If someone makes you mad, stay calm and tell that person how you feel. Then listen to what she has to say. When you follow the Bible's advice, you'll solve your problems fast.

When I get angry, I won't kick or pout—
I'll just do my best to figure things o

Words of Wisdom

The wisdom that comes from heaven is first of all pure;
then peace-loving, considerate, submissive, full of mercy
and good fruit, impartial and sincere.
James 3:17, NIV

TV, movies, and friends can all be full of advice about how to live. But this advice won't always tell you how God wants you to live. So how do you know what to believe? You can use this verse as a little test. God wants you to be kind, to think of others, to show love and forgiveness to people, and to be honest. If anyone tells you to do things that aren't loving or kind, don't pay any attention. Just do what God says, and you'll become wise.

God's path is the only one I should take.
wisdom tells me which choices to make!

Seek God

Come near to God and he will come near to you.
James 4:8, NIV

When you play hide-and-seek, you have to go looking for the person who is hiding. God doesn't hide from us, but we do have to look for him if we want to find him. Just remember, God is always with us. You can feel his love in the good-morning kiss your dad gives you. You can hear his voice in the sound of the wind in the trees. You can see his beauty in the snow, the sunshine, and the big black night. Best of all, he's in your heart, ready for you to find him.

I can't see you, God, but this much I know.
I see your love in the sun, wind, and snow!

Humble Hearts

Humble yourselves before the Lord, and he will lift you up.
James 4:10, NIV

When you're humble, you know you need help sometimes. When a humble person reads a story and gets stuck on a word, she asks for help. When a humble person tries to tie his shoes but can't remember how, he asks for help. Asking for help doesn't mean you're not smart. It really means you're smart enough to know when you can't do something alone. The next time you need help, be humble and ask for it!

God, if I need help with something new,
I'll try to be humble and call on you!

Perfect Answers

The earnest prayer of a righteous person has great power and wonderful results.
James 5:16, NLT

Talking to God is more than just saying words. Praying is the way your heart talks to God. And God always listens. So just believe that God will answer your prayers, and then watch what he does. The answer may not be what you expect, but it will be the perfect answer for you.

God listens to me, heart to heart.
Knowing he'll answer is my favourite part!

All Kinds of People

All of you should live together in peace. Try to understand each other.
1 Peter 3:8, ICB

There are lots of different kinds of people in the world. Just take a look around. Do you know anyone whose skin is a different colour than yours or who speaks a different language? Do you know anyone who can't walk or who can't do all the things you can do? Every person God makes is a little different from every other person God makes. But all people are loved deeply and equally by God. That means you can enjoy all kinds of people, no matter how different they are from you.

**The world's full of people so different from me,
But we're all God's children—and one family!**

Little Helpers

[Help others] with all the strength and energy that God supplies.
I Peter 4:11, NLT

You might think you're too young to really be much help to anyone. After all, you probably still need help with lots of things yourself. But you can be more help than you think! When you play with your little brother, you're helping him feel loved. When you get yourself dressed in the morning, you're helping your parents save time. Every little thing you do for others helps them more than you know.

Though I am young, I can do lots for others.
I can help my parents, my sisters, my brothers.

In the Blink of an Eye

Give all your worries and cares to God,
for he cares about what happens to you.
I Peter 5:7, NLT

Wouldn't it be great
just to blink your eyes
and make all the little
things that worry
you go away? Just
think—no more
being nervous
when your mum
leaves the room,
no more wondering
if anyone will come to
your birthday party. Well, guess what?
You *can* get rid of all your worries in the blink
of an eye. Just give your problems to God and let him
take care of them. You won't have to worry about a thing!

God takes my worries so I can stay calm.
I know he holds me right in his palm!

Sharing God's Gifts

Through his glory and goodness, he gave us the very great and rich gifts
he promised us. With those gifts you can share in being like God.
2 Peter 1:4, ICB

Why do you suppose God promises us so much? One big reason is that he loves us so much. But he also gives us his gifts so that we can be more like him. When you have God's love in your heart and you share it with others, you're doing something God would do. When people hurt you and you forgive them the way God forgives you, you're being like God. When you are patient and kind and joyful, you're sharing God's gifts. God shared all the best parts of himself with us so that we could share them with others.

I love to share God with the people I know,
For when I care, it's God's love that will show.

Telling Time

With the Lord a day is like a thousand years,
and a thousand years are like a day.
2 Peter 3:8, NIV

Did you know that God tells time a lot differently than we do?
Since God's been alive forever, time in heaven isn't the same as
time on earth. When the Bible says God promises to take away
all our sadness and pain, it might not happen
tomorrow or even next week.

It might mean that we
have to wait until we live
in heaven with God. But
no matter how many of our
days it takes for God to keep
his promises, we can trust
that he will.

Many years to God can be like a day.
God tells time in his very own way!

The Light of the World

God is light and there is no darkness in him at all.
I John 1:5, NLT

At this time of year, it starts getting dark much earlier. So what do you do? You turn on some lights. Lights can be very small—as small as a tiny firefly or the flame from a candle on your birthday cake. Some lights are big—they can light up a whole room. But God is the biggest and brightest light there is. He is full of so much light and goodness that there is no darkness in him at all. God's light is so bright, it lights up the whole world!

In God there just isn't anything dark.
God's light is much more than a tiny spark!

A Clear Path

*If we walk in the light as He is in the light, we have fellowship with
one another, and the blood of Jesus Christ His Son
cleanses us from all sin.*
1 John 1:7, NKJV

If you had to choose between walking down a dark, winding path and walking down a brightly lit path where you could see exactly where you were going, which would you choose? Probably the path you could see, right? When we follow God's clear, bright path, we'll find all kinds of good things along the way, like good friends, lots of love, and God's wonderful forgiveness. What a great journey!

When I follow God's way, I'll find lots of joy.
His path is the best for each girl and each boy.

Living for God

If anyone obeys his word, God's love is truly made complete in him.
I John 2:5, NIV

Do you ever wonder if you're doing a good job living for God? if you're being kind enough to the new kid at school? if you're showing enough love to your new stepparent? Well, don't worry. You'll never be perfect when you live on earth. But the good news is that God just wants you to do your best. He wants you to understand how he wants you to live—and then to ask his help doing it!

Following God doesn't have to be tough.
Just do your best—it's really enough!

DECEMBER 17

God's Child

*The Father . . . loved us so much that we are called children of God.
And we really are his children.*
1 John 3:1, ICB

When you are someone's child, it means you're very, very special to them. Just ask your mum or dad. There's no other person in the world who loves you as much. That's why it's so wonderful to be called a child of God. God's not just the one who created you, he's your heavenly Father. And that means he loves you even more than your mum or dad can!

You are God's child, and he really loves you.
Your mum and your dad really love you too!

A New Family

Beloved, now we are children of God.
1 John 3:2, NKJV

Something amazing happens when you love God and trust him. You become one of God's children. You also become part of a great big family of people all over the world. And members of God's family love each other no matter what. They stand up for each other, encourage each other, and help each other. How can you help another one of God's children today?

The world is filled with my sisters and brothers.
Since we're all God's children, we should help each other.

Overflowing Love

We should love each other, because love comes from God.
1 John 4:7, ICB

Have you ever poured too much juice in a cup and accidentally spilled juice all over the table? Well, God's love fills up our hearts the same way. God gives us so much love that our hearts can't hold it all. It spills over to other people. But it's no accident when God's love spills over. In fact, that's just the way God planned it. He gave us all that extra love so we'd have plenty of it to share. Let your love spill out today!

God fills my heart with so much love and care
That it's easy for me to give others a share!

Full of Love

All who live in love live in God, and God lives in them.
1 John 4:16, NLT

After all the Bible verses you've read in this book, you now know how important love is to God. Jesus talked about a lot of interesting things when he lived on the earth. But the thing people remembered most about him was the love he gave. God has done amazing things, like creating the whole universe. But the most important thing he did was send us his Son to show us his love. When you love God and show his love to others, you're living the life God wants for you. It's a life full of love.

God equals love, I know that it's true,
So I can show love to others too!

No More Fear

Where God's love is, there is no fear,
because God's perfect love takes away fear.
1 John 4:18, ICB

We humans can be afraid of some really strange things, like lifts or high places or snakes or spiders. But the more your heart is filled with God's love, the less room there is for fear. You still might not *like* snakes or spiders, but you don't have to be afraid of them. Even more important, you don't have to be afraid of being alone, or of something bad happening to you. God's love can take away all your fear!

When God fills my heart with his wonderful love,
He pushes out fear with a great, mighty shove!

You Are Loved

We love because [God] first loved us.
I John 4:19, NIV

God showed us real love from the moment he created people. He loved Adam so much that he gave him a partner—Eve—so Adam wouldn't be lonely. He loved King David so much that he made him a great king, even though David made some big mistakes. He loved you so much that he sent his Son, Jesus, to live on earth and forgive our mistakes.

Because God first loved us, we can love him back. And we can show his wonderful love to everyone around us, too.

God taught me that love is gentle and kind.
It's a lesson I'll always keep in my mind.

From Beginning to End

"I am ... the Beginning and the Ending of all things," says God, who is the
Lord, the All Powerful One who is, and was, and is coming again!
Revelation 1:8, TLB

God
is our heavenly
Father. And he's also
the Creator of the universe
and everything in it. He created
time, he created heaven, he created
forever, and he created you. When you look
up at the stars, remember where they came from. When you
see a rabbit hopping through your garden, remember who
created it. And when you think about the future, remember
who made it, and who will be with you forever and ever!

God's been around since before time started.
He'll always be with us—we'll never be parted.

Let Jesus In

Look! Here I stand at the door and knock. If you hear me calling and
open the door, I will come in, and we will share a meal as friends.
Revelation 3:20, NLT

Think of your heart like a little house. Now think of Jesus coming to visit. When he knocks on the door, what are you going to do? Will you be too busy to talk to him? Will you tell him to come back later? At Christmas we remember Jesus' birthday and the love God showed us by sending Jesus to live on earth. Jesus wants to be part of your life today and fill you with his love. He's asking to come into your heart and live there forever. Will you let him in?

If you want to have Jesus in your heart,
Letting him in is the best way to start.

Angels Everywhere

I heard the singing of thousands and millions of angels around the throne.
Revelation 5:11, NLT

The very last book of the Bible tells us about an amazing dream. In this dream, John, a man who loved God, saw what heaven might be like. And his dream makes heaven sound like an incredible place. In John's dream, he saw angels in heaven. But not just a few, or even just a few hundred. John heard *millions* of angels singing near God's throne. Can you imagine? What a sound that will be! And *you* will get to hear it!

When I get to heaven, I'll hear angels sing
Many songs to God, our wonderful King.

No More Problems

[The people who have suffered] will never be hungry again.
They will never be thirsty again.
Revelation 7:16, ICB

The world we live in is a very large place. But in some parts of the world, people are very poor. Some people don't have enough food to eat. And some people don't have good water to drink. But one day, every problem we have here on earth will be gone. Even the people who had very hard lives and who were sick or poor or hungry will have everything they need in heaven. That's something to get excited about!

God will take all of our problems away,
When we live with him in heaven one day.

A New World

I saw a new heaven and a new earth.
Revelation 21:1, NIV

In this verse
John was dreaming
about the end of time,
when all of God's people will live together
forever. John says this won't be anything like the life we have
now. Everything we love will be even better, and everything
that causes us pain will be gone. It's hard to imagine living
somewhere other than on earth. But God promises
that our new heavenly home will be better than
our biggest dreams.

Our life in heaven will really be great.
With so many surprises, I hardly can wait!

Streets of Gold

The great street of the city was of pure gold.
Revelation 21:21, NIV

If you were going to make something that people would walk on every day, you probably wouldn't use the most valuable thing you had, would you? But in John's heavenly dream, everything in heaven is so amazing and spectacular that even the streets are made of gold. If heaven has streets that beautiful, just think about what the rest of it will be like!

Heaven is filled with so many great things
That it's no wonder the angels all sing.

Heavenly Days

Nothing evil will be permitted in [heaven].
Revelation 21:27, TLB

Can you imagine having a whole day when nothing but great things happen? Maybe you'd wake up to a sunny day, and your best friend would be waiting outside to play with you. Or you'd get to go to the circus and ride on an elephant. Or you'd get to go to the ocean—in the middle of winter—and swim with a dolphin. Most days aren't filled with that much adventure, but when you get to heaven, you'll have endless days full of happiness. God won't allow bad things into heaven. So your days will be filled with only good times and good feelings!

Heavenly times are waiting for me.
How lovely life in heaven will be!

God's Face

God's servants will worship him. They will see his face.
Revelation 22:3-4, ICB

What do you think God looks like? Does he have a fuzzy beard? Is he taller than your dad? Can God fly? Does he have big muscles? No one knows what God looks like, but one day, you'll find out. When you're in heaven, one of the best things you'll do is see God face-to-face. You'll get to spend time with him, ask him questions, and maybe even hold his hand. Best of all, you'll get to tell God in person how much you love him. And he'll tell you the same.

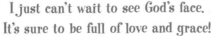
**I just can't wait to see God's face.
It's sure to be full of love and grace!**

DECEMBER 31

Brighter Than the Sun

*There will never be night again. They will not need the light of a lamp or
the light of the sun. The Lord God will give them light.*
Revelation 22:5, ICB

Can you imagine being so close to the sun that you never, ever
need to turn on a light? That's what it will be like to live with
God in heaven. His love is so powerful and so bright, it's even
stronger than the sun. You'll never be afraid of the
dark in heaven because it will never be dark!
God's light will fill
all of heaven
with its warmth
and power.

God's like the sun that shines down on me.
His love is the light that helps me to see!